Financial Liberalization and Macroeconomic Stability

Previous titles in this series:

Financial Liberalization and Macroeconomic Stability

Edited by
Torben M. Andersen
and
Karl O. Moene

BLACKWELL
Publishers

First published as an issue of *The Scandinavian Journal of Economics*
(Vol. 98, No. 4, 1996)

Blackwell Publishers
108 Cowley Road, Oxford OX4 1JF, UK
and
350 Main Street,
Malden, MA 02148, USA

British Library Cataloguing in Publication Data applied for

Library of Congress Cataloguing in Publication Data applied for

ISBN 978-0-631-20349-0

Contents

Financial Liberalization and Macroeconomic Stability

Editors' Preface

Most advanced countries have recently deregulated their credit markets and international capital movements have been liberalized. Over the same period, we have also experienced volatile financial markets and exchange rate crises, particularly in a number of European countries. This naturally raises the question of whether financial liberalization has affected macroeconomic stability and, if so, through which channels. This volume brings together theoretical and empirical contributions addressing these issues.

As capital markets are liberalized, exchange rate crises may become more contagious. In their contribution, *Barry Eichengreen, Andrew Rose* and *Charles Wyplosz* offer empirical evidence indicating that this has been underlying the recent crises in the European currency market. This phenomenon has renewed interest in the fundamental factors determining credibility of exchange rate policies, as explored by *Steinar Holden* and *Birger Vikøren*, and whether a Tobin tax on foreign exchange transactions could mute speculative pressure and stabilize the international monetary system, as analyzed by *Olivier Jeanne*. Macroeconomic stability towards different types of shocks may change as a result of both further capital market integration, emphasized in *Alan Sutherland*'s paper, and monetary arrangements related to exchange rate management, highlighted in the contribution by *Matthew B. Canzoneri* and *Harris Dellas*. This also raises the question, discussed by *Asbjørn Rødseth*, of how the choice of operating targets for monetary policy affects output stability. Seen from a single country perspective, capital market liberalization has had its most important effects by facilitating households' access to credit markets, analyzed in the paper by *Jonas Agell* and *Lennart Berg*, and opening up financial markets to foreign investors, examined in *Peter Sellin*'s contribution.

Financial support from the Karl Langenskiöld Fund, Royal Swedish Academy of Sciences, Stockholm, is gratefully acknowledged.

Torben M. Andersen
Karl O. Moene

Contagious Currency Crises: First Tests*

Barry Eichengreen

University of California, Berkeley, CA 94720-3880, USA

Andrew Rose

University of California, Berkeley 94720-1990, USA

Charles Wyplosz

Graduate Institute of International Studies, CH-1211 Geneva, Switzerland

Abstract

We address the fact that the incidence of speculative attacks tends to be temporally correlated; that is, currency crises appear to pass "contagiously" from one country to another. The paper provides a survey of the theoretical literature. We also provide empirical evidence consistent with the contagious nature of currency crises. We estimate that the existence of a currency crisis elsewhere in the world (whether successful or not) raises the probability of an attack on the domestic currency by 8 percent, even after taking account of a variety of domestic political and economic factors.

I. Introduction

The scope for currency crises to spill contagiously across countries has been hotly debated in the wake of the Mexican meltdown. A frequently cited justification for the $50 billion of assistance provided by the IMF, the U.S. and other G-7 governments in early 1995 was that the effects of the Mexican crisis, if allowed to play themselves out, would not be limited to that country; rather, other emerging markets would have experienced serious repercussions. Because the Mexican authorities had little incentive to internalize these externalities, multilateral intervention was justified. In support of this view observers cite the reserve losses, interest-rate increases and weakening exchange rates suffered by countries like Argentina and Thailand in the early weeks of 1995. The contrary view is that investors were discriminating in the countries they attacked. Currencies other than the Mexican peso were subjected to relatively little pressure, and only countries with large current-account deficits, overvalued real rates and other weak fundamentals felt much of an effect. The implication is that the

* We thank Shirish Gupta for research assistance, the editors for comments, and the National Science Foundation (Economics Division) for financial support.

Mexican bailout, to the extent that it was justified by fears of contagion, was uncalled for.

A similar controversy arose at the time of the 1992–93 crises in the European Monetary System. In 1992 it was argued that the French franc and the Irish punt came under attack as a result of the earlier crises experienced by the British pound and the Italian lira. In 1993 it was argued that the attack on the French franc threatened to spill over to other European currencies. The implication drawn was that foreign support of the franc was essential to prevent chaos from spreading contagiously throughout the EMS. The rebuttal was that only European countries whose fundamentals were weak were subjected to speculative attacks; others like the Netherlands remained immune because they appropriately aligned their economic policies to the maintenance of their currency pegs. If contagion existed, the implication went, only countries in particular economic and political circumstances were susceptible.

Clearly, the stakes for policy are immense. Ascertaining whether there exists contagion in foreign exchange markets and under what conditions contagious currency crises arise should be a high priority for empirical research in open-economy macroeconomics. It is remarkable therefore that there exists little systematic analysis of the question. Our goal in this appear is to take a first step towards filling this gap.

We use a panel of quarterly data for 20 industrial countries for the period 1959–93 to test for contagious currency crises. We ask whether the probability of a crisis in a country at a point in time is correlated with the incidence of crises in other countries at the same time, after controlling for the effects of political and economic fundamentals. The evidence is striking: a variety of tests and a battery of sensitivity analyses uniformly suggest that a crisis elsewhere in the world increases the probability of a speculative attack by an economically and statistically significant amount (our best estimate is eight percentage points), even after controlling for economic and political fundamentals in the country concerned. This would appear to be the first systematic evidence of the existence of contagious currency crises.

The remainder of our paper is organized as follows. Section II provides an overview of the theoretical literature on speculative attacks in foreign exchange markets, with special reference to contagion. Section III reviews related empirical studies. In Section IV we present new evidence on contagion. Section V concludes.

II. Theories of Speculative Attacks, Contagious and Otherwise

In this section we review the theoretical literature on speculative attacks in foreign exchange markets, starting with the seminal Krugman (1979) model, proceeding to models of multiple equilibria, and concluding with models of contagious currency crises.[1]

Speculative Attacks

Krugman's contribution was to show how inconsistencies between domestic economic conditions and an exchange rate commitment lead to the collapse of the currency peg. In his model, the overly expansionary stance of domestic policy causes domestic absorption to exceed production. The difference spills over into a balance-of-payments deficit, which the central bank finances by expending reserves. Eventually reserves fall to a critical threshold at which a speculative attack is launched, eliminating the authorities' remaining foreign assets. Once reserves are depleted, the exchange rate peg is abandoned, and the currency depreciates secularly over time, reflecting the more expansionary stance of policy at home than abroad.

This theory of balance of payments crises has produced four classes of insights. First, it helps to identify the relevant fundamentals. Most obviously, these should include macroeconomic determinants of the exchange rate and the balance of payments, as embodied in aggregative models of exchange rate determination and the literature on the monetary approach to the balance of payments. Given the forward-looking nature of these models, this list of determinants will necessarily include expected future values of the relevant series.[2] At the same time, the poor empirical performance of these models gives grounds for concern about the success with which speculative-attack models building on these foundations can be implemented empirically; we revisit this point below.[3]

Second, the Krugman model demonstrates how crises can erupt before official reserves, which decline secularly over time, actually hit zero. Currency speculation takes the form of purchases and sales of domestic currency for foreign assets. Those transactions arise as traders exchange assets among themselves so as to equalize rates of return and, more generally, to balance their portfolios, trading off risk and return. They provoke a crisis when no one in the market is willing to acquire domestic currency at the prevailing price (given by the pegged rate of exchange). Under these circumstances, the only counterpart on the short side of the market is the central bank. Speculators have an incentive to liquidate their holdings of domestic currency while the central bank retains sufficient

---

[1] A recent survey is Blackburn and Sola (1993).
[2] That expected future fundamentals can themselves depend on whether a speculative attack occurs is what gives rise to the possibility of multiple equilibria, as we explain below.
[3] For evidence and surveys of the empirical performance of this class of models, see Meese and Rogoff (1983), Obstfeld and Rogoff (1995) and Obstfeld (1995).

reserves to absorb the volume of sales. The timing of the attack is determined such that its magnitude just suffices to eliminate the central bank's entire stock of reserves.

A third implication of the basic model is that the central bank can only maintain a currency peg if it possesses adequate foreign exchange reserves. Once their reserves have been lost in the attack, the authorities have no choice but to abandon the peg. In the standard model, crises thus result in a transition to floating. The model thus implies that reserve stocks must be reconstituted before the exchange rate can be re-pegged. The standard formulation also helps us think about the meaning of "reserve adequacy". To defend the currency peg, the central bank must be capable of purchasing all of its liabilities that are put up for sale by other agents. In the standard model, the volume of sales is small: it corresponds to the decline in monetary base needed to ratify the fall in money demand associated with the higher interest rates that prevail following the shift from a pegged to a depreciating exchange rate. Normally, domestic residents continue to hold a significant proportion of the base following the collapse of the peg, since they need it for transactions purposes. But in highly dollarized economies, the transactions demand for domestic currency can be very small, as pointed out by, *inter alia*, Edwards (1989); in this case, the share of the monetary base subject to liquidation in a crisis may be quite large. More worrisome still is the possibility that the monetary authorities will also be required to purchase other domestic liabilities (i.e., M2) if the currency crisis provokes a banking crisis.[4]

A fourth implication of the standard model is that the authorities have little chance of fending off an attack. Even if the volume of speculative sales of domestic currency is less than the monetary base, the base still exceeds the net stock of foreign reserves of the central bank (except in very special circumstances like a fully backed currency board). In principle, the authorities can augment their gross reserves by borrowing abroad, possibly to the point where reserves exceed the base. But if borrowed reserves are used to finance sterilized intervention, the monetary base increases *pari passu*, and there is no level of gross reserves sufficient to repel an attack. If the authorities do not sterilize, then the attack can be repelled, but only at the cost of allowing the base to shrink and interest rates to rise. If a sizable proportion of the base is involved, the resulting interest rate increases may be so large that the exchange rate crisis precipitates a banking crisis. To avert the latter, the central bank may then have to resume sterilizing its

---

[4] The link between financial and exchange crises is emphasized by Goldfajn and Valdés (1995) and is a point to which we return below.

intervention, which will again undermine its capacity to defend the currency peg.

Multiple Equilibria

A generic feature of theoretical macroeconomic models with rational expectations is that such models typically have multiple solutions. Since most of these solution paths do not converge to a steady state, standard practice for many years was to assume away divergent solutions by invoking transversality conditions. More recently however this non-uniqueness property — which allows for multiple equilibria — has become the basis for a literature on speculative bubbles and sun-spot equilibria. Obstfeld (1986, 1995), following a suggestion by Flood and Garber (1984), has provided examples of multiple equilibria and self-fulfilling attacks in foreign exchange markets. These offer a wholly new perspective on the causes of currency crises.

The possibility of multiple equilibria arises when market participants, while not questioning that current policy is compatible with the indefinite maintenance of the currency peg, anticipate that a successful attack will alter policy. In these circumstances, it is expected future fundamentals, conditional on an attack taking place, rather than current fundamentals and expected future fundamentals absent an attack, which are incompatible with the peg. Two equilibria thus exist: the first one features no attack, no change in fundamentals, and indefinite maintenance of the peg; the second one features a speculative attack followed by a change in fundamentals which validates, *ex post*, the exchange-rate change that speculators expected to take place.

In Obstfeld (1986), pre- and post-crisis policies are set arbitrarily. If an attack occurs, the government is simply assumed to shift policy in a more expansionary direction. The arbitrary nature of this contingent policy process is the obvious limitation of the model. Subsequently, Bensaid and Jeanne (1993), Ozkan and Sutherland (1995) and Obstfeld (1995) have proposed models of optimizing governments which find it in their self interest to follow the kind of contingent policy processes that can give rise to multiple equilibria and self-fulfilling attacks. Their analyses build on the literature on exchange rate escape clauses, in which it is optimal to maintain the currency peg under some circumstances and to abandon it under others; see Obstfeld (1991), De Kock and Grilli (1994) and Drazen and Masson (1994).

In these models, the behaviour of governments still derives from special utility functions. In this sense, the literature on multiple equilibria and self-fulfilling attacks in foreign exchange markets is merely a collection of examples and special cases. This point is emphasized by Krugman (1996), who establishes two further results. First, he suggests that multiple equilibria are, paradoxically, less likely when the fundamentals are wrong. When fundamentals are clearly inconsistent with the prevailing currency peg, investors have little doubt that a crisis will ultimately occur, and the model quickly converges to the equilibrium in which the currency is attacked and devalued; only when fundamentals are "good enough" that there remains uncertainty about whether a crisis will eventually result do there exist multiple equilibria. Second, Krugman shows that if the public does not know the authorities preferences, there may be "testing" by the markets — that is, one may observe attacks that are unsuccessful but which reveal information about the preferences of the authorities.[5]

Models of self-fulfilling attacks imply that "good" fundamentals may not suffice to avert currency crises. To prevent an attack unjustified by fundamentals, the credibility of the central bank must be such that markets rule out a relaxation of policy once the peg is abandoned. Obstfeld (1986) provides such an example: there, the expectation that the central bank will react to a crisis by implementing a policy which implies an exchange rate appreciation eliminates the risk of a self-fulfilling crisis.

Contagion

Very little theoretical work has analyzed the conditions under which currency crises can spread contagiously across countries. The first systematic theoretical treatment of this question was Gerlach and Smets (1995). Inspired by the links between the fall of the Finnish markka in 1992 and the subsequent attack on the Swedish krona, they consider two countries linked together by trade in merchandise and financial assets. In their model, a successful attack on one exchange rate leads to its real depreciation, which enhances the competitiveness of the country's merchandise exports. This produces a trade deficit in the second country, a gradual decline in the international reserves of its central bank, and ultimately an attack on its currency. A second channel for contagious transmission is the impact of crisis and depreciation in the first country on the import prices and the overall price level in the second. Post-crisis real depreciation in the first country reduces import prices in the second. In turn, this reduces its

---

[5] While testing is not, strictly speaking, an example of self-fulfilling attacks since markets anticipations are not fulfilled, it is a case where the attack is unjustified by the fundamentals.

consumer price index and the demand for money by its residents. Their efforts to swap domestic currency for foreign exchange then deplete the foreign reserves of the central bank. This may shift the second economy from a no-attack equilibrium, in which reserves more than suffice to absorb the volume of prospective speculative sales and in which there consequently exist no grounds for a speculative attack, to a second equilibrium in which an attack can succeed and in which speculators thus have an incentive to launch it.[6]

Buiter *et al.* (1996) use an escape-clause model of exchange rate policy to analyze the spread of currency crises in a system of $N + 1$ countries, N of which (denoted the "periphery") peg to the remaining country (the "center"). The center is more risk averse than the others and is hence unwilling to pursue a cooperative monetary policy designed to stabilize exchange rates. A negative shock to the center which leads it to raise interest rates then induces the members of the periphery to reconsider their currency-pegging policy. If the members of the periphery cooperate, they may find it collectively optimal to leave the system — an extreme case of contagion. More generally, some subset of peripheral countries — those with the least tolerance for high interest rates — will find it optimal to leave the system under these circumstances, and contagion will be limited to this subset. Importantly, however, their decision to leave stabilizes the currency pegs of the remaining members of the system, because monetary expansion and currency depreciation by some members of the periphery provides an incentive for the center country, which now finds itself with an increasingly overvalued exchange rate, to relax its monetary stance, relieving the pressure on rest of the periphery. In this model, contagion is selective: the shock to the center spills over negatively to some members of the periphery but positively to others.

Another paper provides an analysis of contagious currency crises is Goldfajn and Valdés (1995). They focus on the role of illiquidity in finan-

---

[6] A similar argument is developed by Andersen (1994), building on escape-clause models of exchange-rate policy. In his model, the government is prompted to abandon its currency peg by a shock coming from outside the currency market. An exogenous deterioration in domestic competitiveness which increases domestic unemployment, for example, may give the authorities an incentive to opt for a more expansionary policy which reduced unemployment through surprise inflation, *à la* Barro and Gordon (1983). Andersen argues that his model provides a plausible description of exchange rate policy in Northern Europe in 1991–92, when the collapse of Soviet trade with the Nordic countries first aggravated unemployment in Finland, leading its government to adopt a more expansionary policy which required abandoning the currency peg, and which then spilled over to the exchange rates of the rest of Scandinavia.

cial markets. A key feature of their model is the introduction of financial intermediaries. These authors show how, in the presence of such intermediaries, small disturbances can provoke large-scale runs on a currency. Intermediaries supply liquid assets to foreigners unwilling to commit to long-term investments; that is, they provide maturity-transformation services. By offering attractive terms on liquid deposits, their presence augments the volume of capital inflow. But when, for exogenous reasons, foreign investors withdraw their deposits, intermediaries unable to cost-lessly liquidate their assets face the risk of failure. Hence, a bank run can produce a self-fulfilling banking crisis, cf. Diamond and Dibvig (1983), in the same way that a run on the currency can provoke a self-fulfilling exchange-rate crisis. Moreover, the run on intermediaries can spill over into a run on the currency as foreign investors withdraw their deposits and convert them into foreign exchange. These crises can spread contagiously to other countries when international investors encountering liquidity difficulties as a result of the banking crisis in one country respond by liquidating their positions in other national markets.

A related literature concerned with information, while not directly concerned with contagion in foreign exchange markets, provides a complementary approach to the issue. Shiller (1995) provides a model in which financial market participants share access to much of the same information (e.g. that which appears on Reuters screens) but interpret and process it in different ways. What they make of their shared information depends on their own experience, which in turn is shaped by local conditions which only they experience. Consequently, one market's reaction to a piece of new information can provide a signal about its global implications. It may suggest to traders in other markets how they too should react. The fact that one market draws dramatic conclusions from some information may overcome local culture in other markets and lead to a revision of expectations (an "information cascade"). In the present context, one can see how this effect could lead an attack on one exchange rate to prompt traders in other currency markets to attack those exchange rates as well.

A similar analysis, also based on informational issues, is Caplin and Leahy (1995). In their model, financial market participants expect a crisis but have diffuse priors over its timing. It is costly for traders to take a position in advance of a crisis, in other words to move too early. Each trader is unsure whether others share his or her belief that a crisis will eventually occur. They exchange "cheap talk" amongst themselves but draw inferences only from positions taken in the market. The result is normal market conditions ("business as usual") with no hint of crisis until it suddenly erupts. Once it occurs, however, market participants all claim that they knew that the crisis was about to happen and that they were readying themselves for the eventuality (they display "wisdom after the fact"). This model can give rise to contagion insofar as a crisis somewhere in the world confirms individually-held suspicions in other markets.[7]

III. Empirical Studies of Speculative Attacks, Contagious and Otherwise

While the literature on crises in foreign exchange markets is replete with models that highlight motives for and dynamics of speculative attacks, the process of systematically testing the predictions of those theories has barely begun. We put the emphasis in this last sentence on the word "systematically". Otherwise convincing studies of currency crises frequently assemble evidence from biased samples of episodes. It is not just that they consider a selective sample of episodes in which currency pegs collapsed without confirming that the collapses they analyze are representative of the underlying population. It is that episodes in which pegs were abandoned are themselves unrepresentative of the population of speculative attacks. Some pegs are abandoned without a speculative attack. Others are repelled. Thus, studies like Dornbusch, Goldfajn and Valdés (1995) and Krugman (1996), while informative about the characteristics of the episodes they consider, do not provide a representative characterization of speculative attacks.

In Eichengreen, Rose and Wyplosz (1995) we seek to analyze currency crises systematically by constructing a measure of speculative attacks that excludes devaluations and flotations not taken in a climate of crisis and includes unsuccessful attacks. We compare these with actual devaluations and other changes in exchange rate arrangements. Our measure of crises is a weighted average of changes in the exchange rate, changes in international reserves which can be paid out in response to speculative pressure, and changes in the interest differential since interest rates can be raised to fend off an attack. (A more detailed description of the methodology is presented below.) We analyze the experience of some two dozen OECD economies since 1959.

Our findings on the causes and consequences of devaluations and revaluations are consistent with the predictions of mainstream models. Countries which devalue experience problems of external balance in the

---

[7] An illustrative application of this model would be to the ERM crises of 1992–93. The story would go as follows. There was a widespread belief at the time that the ERM could not continue to operate indefinitely without a realignment. And yet its extraordinary stability since January 1987 led traders to accept the official view that the system could now function without further realignments. Extraneous circumstances (the political difficulties of ratifying the Maastricht Treaty) then triggered a crisis (which culminated in the devaluation of the Italian lira) which confirmed this belief. It revealed to all traders that what they privately believed all along was true — that realignments were still necessary.

period leading up to the event. Their trade deficits and reserve losses are associated with relatively expansionary monetary policies. In addition, the period leading up to devaluations is characterized by problems of internal balance as reflected in relatively high levels of unemployment; the expansionary monetary stance in these countries may be adopted partly in response to these domestic concerns. Broadly speaking, revaluations are mirror images of devaluations.[8] Other events in foreign exchange markets, in contrast, resist generalization. For example, transitions between exchange rate regimes (like movements from fixed to floating rates) are largely unpredictable.

We find that countries susceptible to crises are those whose governments have pursued accommodating monetary policies leading to high inflation and reserve losses, generally in response to deteriorating conditions on the unemployment front. Initially, the current account moves into deficit, and the capital account worsens as the crisis nears. Countries which take last-minute steps to defend the currency by significantly reducing the rate of money growth sometimes succeed in defending the rate. Those which retrench less dramatically may still be forced to capitulate but often do so without provoking a major crisis. In contrast, governments which rely on sterilized intervention to the exclusion of more fundamental policy adjustments are generally unable to avoid full-blown currency crises.

A few other studies have adopted this approach. For example, Moreno (1995) analyzes crises in the Pacific Basin economies from 1980 through 1994. He finds that periods of speculative pressure tend to be associated with large budget deficits and rapid rates of growth of domestic credit. There is some evidence that episodes of pressure arise when slow growth and relatively high inflation make it difficult for the government to maintain a stable exchange rate. In contrast, there is no evidence that indicators of external balance differ between crises and tranquil periods.

Kaminsky and Reinhart (1996) consider speculative attacks on currencies and banking crises, analyzing connections between the two. They focus on 20 countries in Asia, Europe, Latin America and the Middle East that experienced banking difficulties in the period 1970–95. Their index of currency crises is constructed as a weighted average of exchange rate changes and reserve changes (because the relevant interest rate data are lacking for some countries). In their sample, crises tend to be preceded by declining economic activity, weakening export sectors, falling stock

---

[8] This evidence is consistent with models emphasizing the domestic determinants of external balance as well as with more recent models which focus instead on the decisions of governments concerned with internal balance and constrained by the exchange rate in their choice of policy response.

markets, and high real interest rates. In addition, crises are preceded by accelerating money growth and rapid rates of growth of the liabilities of the banking system. Banking crises are leading indicators of currency crises, but there are few instances where currency crises predict banking crises.

By comparison, empirical analyses of contagion are few. Typical of the literature are studies which provide informal comparisons of small groups of countries. Burki and Edwards (1995) contrast the experiences of Argentina, Brazil and Venezuela in the wake of the Mexican crisis with those of Chile and Colombia, suggesting that contagion, while present, was selective. Calvo (1996) provides a series of comparisons between Mexico and other countries in an effort to understand why some countries were more susceptible than others to the tequila effect.

We are aware of two statistical studies of contagion. Calvo and Reinhart (1995) report evidence of contagion in an econometric model in which capital flows to four small Latin American countries depend on the standard determinants but also on a contagion proxy, namely, capital flows to four large Latin American countries. Their results can be questioned, however, on the grounds that the flow of capital to neighboring countries is a less-than-ideal proxy for contagion and that the sample of countries is not random.

Schmukler and Frankel (1996) model contagion using data on closed-end country funds. Although their dependent variable, the level of stock prices, is different from the one with which we are concerned, the two are linked insofar as the rise in domestic interest rates needed to fend off an attack on the currency will tend to depress equity prices.[9] Their evidence suggests that investors differentiated among countries to a greater extent after the 1994 Mexican crisis than after its 1982 predecessor. In the short run, a drop in Mexican prices tends to induce sell-offs in other markets motivated by the desire to raise cash; while there is evidence of contagion in Latin America in the long run as well, the long-run effect of a Mexican sell-off on Asian markets is positive.[10]

---

[9] Linkages between the stock market and the exchange rate are analyzed by Murphy (1989).

[10] In a similar exercise, Valdés (1996) analyzes the secondary market prices of sovereign debt and shows that there exists a strong cross-country correlation of these prices even after controlling for macroeconomic fundamentals and "big news events" such as announcements of Brady Plan restructurings. This evidence of "contagion" in the markets for developing-country debt is much stronger than analogous evidence for the U.S. corporate bond market, where fundamentals explain essentially all of the observed correlation across issues, and than in a group of medium-sized OECD countries, where fundamentals again explain all of the observed correlation of credit ratings.

IV. Analyzing Contagion Systematically

We now test for the existence of "contagious" currency crises. The contagion effect with which we are concerned can be thought of as an increase in the probability of a speculative attack on the domestic currency which stems not from domestic "fundamentals" such as money and output but from the existence of a (not necessarily successful) speculative attack elsewhere in the world.

We analyze a panel of quarterly macroeconomic and political data covering twenty industrial countries from 1959 through 1993 (a total of 2800 observations). We pose the following question: is the incidence of a currency crisis in a particular country at a given point in time (e.g., France in the third quarter of 1992) correlated with the incidence of a currency crisis in a different country (e.g., the U.K.) at the same point in time, even after taking into account the effects of current and lagged domestic macroeconomic and political influences? The finding of a strong positive partial correlation is consistent with the existence of contagion, since it implies that speculative attacks are temporally correlated even after conditioning on domestic factors. Still, it is difficult to interpret this as definitive proof of contagion, since it may in fact reflect not contagion but an unmeasured common shock to economic fundamentals which strikes a number of countries simultaneously, rather than actual spillovers from one country to another.[11]

Measuring Currency Crises

The first issue that must be confronted is how to determine when a speculative attack has occurred. Having addressed this issue in a number of previous papers, e.g. Eichengreen, Rose and Wyplosz (1995, 1996), we provide only a summary of our thinking here.

Currency crises cannot be identified with actual devaluations, revaluations and instances in which the currency is floated, for two reasons.[12] First, not all speculative attacks are successful. The currency may be supported through the expenditure of reserves by the central bank or by foreign central banks and governments.[13] Alternatively, the authorities may repel attacks by raising interest rates and adopting other policies of austerity. Further, many realignments are taken deliberately in tranquil periods, possibly to preclude future attacks.

---

[11] We return to this point below.
[12] We refer to such actual changes in explicit exchange rate policy as "events" and think of them as overlapping in part with the currency crises that we are interested in.
[13] And occasionally by the actual or threatened imposition of capital controls.

Ideally, an index of speculative pressure would be obtained by employing a structural model of exchange rate determination, from which one would derive the excess demand for foreign exchange. In practice, however, empirical models linking macroeconomic variables to the exchange rate have little explanatory power at short and intermediate horizons.[14] In the absence of an empirically valid macro-model, we resort to an *ad hoc* approach, the underlying intuition for which is derived from the well-known model of exchange market pressure due to Girton and Roper (1977). The idea is that an excess demand for foreign exchange can be met through several (not mutually exclusive) channels. If the attack is successful, depreciation or devaluation occurs. But the monetary authorities may instead accommodate the pressure by running down their international reserves or deter the attack by raising interest rates. As a measure of speculative pressure, we therefore construct a weighted average of exchange rate changes, reserve changes, and interest rate changes. All of these variables are measured relative to those prevailing in Germany, the reference country. Germany is a logical choice for a center country, since it has had a strong currency throughout the postwar era, and has been a critical member of all important OECD fixed exchange rate systems (including the Bretton Woods System, the EMS, and the "snake" preceding the EMS).[15]

The index of exchange market pressure then becomes:

$$\text{EMP}_{i,t} \equiv [(\alpha \% \Delta e_{i,t}) + (\beta \Delta (i_{i,t} - i_{G,t})) - (\gamma (\% \Delta r_{i,t} - \% \Delta r_{G,t}))],$$

where $e_{i,t}$ denotes the price of a DM in i's currency at time t; i_G denotes the short German interest; r denotes the ratio of international reserves;[16] and α, β, and γ are weights.

We define crises as extreme values of this index.

$$\text{Crisis}_{i,t} = 1 \quad \text{if } \text{EMP}_{i,t} > 1.5\sigma_{\text{EMP}} + \mu_{\text{EMP}}$$

$$= 0 \quad \text{otherwise,}$$

where μ_{EMP} and σ_{EMP} are the sample mean and standard deviation of EMP, respectively.

A critical step is weighting the three components of the index. An obvious option is an unweighted average, which has the advantage of simplicity. But since the volatility of reserves, exchange rates and interest

---

[14] Frankel and Rose (1995) provide a recent survey.

[15] Of course, idiosyncratic German shocks then acquire disproportionate importance. However, German unification is typically considered to be the only important such shock; our sensitivity analysis indicates that our results do not stem from this event.

[16] Following Girton and Roper (1977), r is actually the ratio of reserves to narrow money (M1).

differential is very different, we instead weight the components so as to equalize the volatilities of the three components, thereby preventing any one of them from dominating the index. Below, we check the sensitivity of our results to this scheme.

We identify quarters in which our index of speculative pressure is at least one and a half standard deviations above the sample mean as instances of speculative attacks (although we again test for sensitivity with respect to this arbitrarily-chosen threshold). To avoid counting the same crisis more than once, we exclude the later observation(s) when two (or more) crises occur in successive quarters. Thus, our "exclusion window" is one quarter (though again we vary this parameter). We refer to our non-crisis observations as "tranquil" periods and use these as the control group.[17]

Our choices of a one quarter exclusion window (so that each country contributes no more than two observations annually) and a 1.5 standard deviation outlier threshold produce a sample of 77 crises and 1179 periods of tranquility.[18]

The crisis observations are not randomly distributed. There are clusters of speculative attacks in 1973 (at the time of the breakup of the Bretton Woods system) and in 1992 (at the time of the European currency crises). A time-series plot of the number of crises in each quarter is provided as Figure 1.

Crises Per Quarter

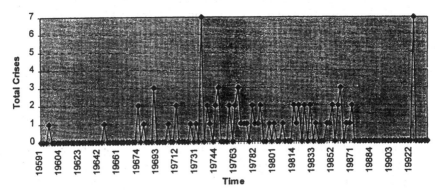

Fig. 1.

---

[17] Just as we do not allow crises in successive quarters to count as independent observations by excluding the latter, we also do not allow two successive periods of tranquility to count as independent observations. We do this by applying our exclusion window to periods of both crisis and tranquility.

[18] However, missing data will preclude use of some of these observations.

The Data

Most of the financial and macroeconomic variables are taken from the CD-ROM version of the International Monetary Fund's *International Financial Statistics* (IFS). The data set is quarterly, spanning 1959 through 1993 for twenty industrial countries.[19] It has been checked for transcription and other errors and corrected. Most of the variables are transformed into differential percentage changes by taking differences between domestic and German annualized fourth-differences of natural logarithms and multiplying by a hundred.

We employ the following variables: total non-gold international reserves (IFS line 1ld); period-average exchange rates (line rf); short-term interest rates (money market rates (line 60b) where possible, discount rates otherwise (line 60)); exports and imports (both measured in dollars, lines 70d and 71d, respectively); the current account (line 77a.d, converted to domestic currency) and the central government budget position (line 80), both measured as percentages of nominal GDP (frequently line 99a); long-term government bond yields (line 61); a nominal stock market index (line 62, which sets 1990 = 100); domestic credit (line 32); M1 (line 34); M2 (line 35 + M1); the CPI (line 64); and real GDP (usually line 99a.r). We also use the real effective exchange rate as a measure of competitiveness (line reu, which uses normalized relative unit labor costs), though this variable is only available from 1975.

We also utilize a number of labor market indicators not included in IFS. Data on total employment, the unemployment rate, and the business sector wage rate were drawn from the OECD's *Main Economic Indicators*. To capture political conditions we construct indicators of governmental electoral victories and defeats, using Keesing's *Record of World Events* and Banks' *Political Handbook of the World*.

Finally, we use a list of exchange market "events" (devaluations, flotations, changes in exchange rate band widths and so forth). These are gleaned from the IMF's annual report on *Exchange Arrangements and Exchange Restrictions*. These volumes also provide us the basis for constructing with dummy variables indicating the presence of capital controls.

The available data on international reserves are less than ideal for a number of well-known reasons. Off-balance sheet transactions, third-party intervention, stand-by credits, and foreign liabilities, all of which are relevant for foreign exchange intervention, tend to be omitted or incom-

---

[19] The countries in our sample include (in order of IMF country number): the U.S., U.K., Austria, Belgium, Denmark, France, Italy, Netherlands, Norway, Sweden, Switzerland, Canada, Japan, Finland, Greece, Ireland, Portugal, Spain and Australia, along with our center country, Germany.

pletely reported. In addition, short-duration attacks (especially unsuccessful ones) may not be evident in quarterly data. Finally, subtle changes in actual or anticipated capital controls, while difficult to measure, may in fact be quite important, especially when countries are mounting defenses against speculative attacks.

Statistical Analysis

We can now test for the existence of contagion. We test the null hypothesis that the incidence of currency crises elsewhere in the world at the same point in time does not affect the probability of a speculative attack on the domestic currency. While our model attempts to control for the influence of a wide range of current and lagged macroeconomic variables, it is non-structural. This is one reason for viewing our evidence (which turns out to be inconsistent with the null at standard confidence levels) as consistent with, but not definitive proof of, contagion.

We estimate a binary probit model, linking our dependent variable (an indicator variable which takes on a value of unity for a speculative attack and zero otherwise) to our controls with maximum likelihood, including additional regressors to capture the effects of macroeconomic and political influences which affect crisis incidence. We cast our net as widely as possible, including: (1) the presence of capital controls; (2) electoral victory or defeat of the government; (3) the growth of domestic credit; (4) inflation; (5) output growth; (6) employment growth; (7) the unemployment rate; (8) the central government budget surplus (+) or deficit (−), expressed as a percentage of GDP; and (9) the current account surplus/ deficit (again, a percentage of GDP). All these variables are included as deviations from German values.

Since the literature on currency crises does not provide much guidance about the time horizon for these influences, we consider a range of plausible alternatives. At the short end of the spectrum, we allow only contemporary influences to affect the probability of a crisis. We then allow for explanatory variables lagged up to two quarters, one year, and two years. We allow these lagged influences to operate jointly with the contemporaneous variables or by themselves (as would be appropriate if lags in data collection or processing preclude the consideration of contemporaneous developments). To conserve degrees of freedom, we model the lags using moving averages. Rather than including the first and second lags of inflation separately, for example, we include only a single term which is the average inflation differential in the two preceding quarters.

This leads us to estimate the following model:

$$\text{Crisis}_{i,t} = \omega D(\text{Crisis}_{j,t}) + \lambda I(L)_{i,t} + \varepsilon_{i,t}$$

where

$D(\text{Crisis}_{j,t}) = 1$ if $\text{Crisis}_{j,t} = 1$,   for any $j \neq i$

           $= 0$ otherwise,

and where $I(L)_{i,t}$ is an information set of ten contemporaneous and/or lagged control regressors; λ is the corresponding vector of nuisance coefficients; and ε is a normally distributed disturbance representing a host of omitted influences which affect the probability of a currency crisis.

The null of interest is H_0: $\omega = 0$. We interpret evidence of the null as being inconsistent with a contagion effect.

Results

Benchmark results are presented in Table 1. Its five columns correspond to five assumptions about the appropriate time horizon for the regressors. Since probit coefficients are not easily interpretable, we report the effects of one-unit (percentage point) changes in the regressors on the probability of a crisis (also expressed in percentage points), evaluated at the mean of the data. We tabulate the associated z-statistics, which test the null of no effect. Statistics which are inconsistent with the null at the five percent level are printed in bold. Diagnostics are reported at the foot of the table, including a test for the joint significance of all the coefficients.

The results are consistent with the existence of a contagion effect which is economically important and statistically significant. A speculative attack elsewhere in the world increases the probability of a domestic currency crisis by around eight percentage points.

The impact of the other regressors is not dramatic, though a few effects are worth noting. For example, higher inflation and unemployment are associated with increases in the odds of an attack. Generally speaking, however, the absence of robust partial correlations provides grounds for caution against over-interpreting the results.

Sensitivity analysis is reported in Table 2. We consider six perturbations of our basic model. First, we change the definition of a speculative attack by raising the outlier threshold on our exchange market pressure index to two standard deviations (from one and a half) and by widening the exclusion band width to two quarters (from one). This marginally increases the magnitude of the contagion variable, although the change is not statistically significant. Second, we change the definition of a speculative attack by doubling the weight on actual exchange rate changes in our tripartite index. This has no discernible impact on the coefficient on the contagion variable. Third, we drop post-1978 data so as to focus on the pre-EMS period. This increases the magnitude of the contagion coefficient further.

Fourth, we limit the sample to EMS observations; here we get strikingly large contagion effects, with slope derivatives almost three times the size of the benchmark result in the first column of Table 1. Fifth, we employ only observations where capital controls are present. Here, the coefficient on the contagion variable is indistinguishable from the benchmark result. Finally, we substitute for crises elsewhere in the world exchange market "events" elsewhere in the world (e.g., actual devaluation or transitions to floating rates), a perturbation which leaves the baseline results relatively unaffected. These tests confirm the key finding of this paper. Namely, a speculative attack elsewhere in the world significantly increases the odds of an attack on the domestic currency. But they do not allow us to distinguish among the various theories of contagion. For example, the relatively large

Table 1. *Probit results*

	Contem-poraneous	MA of Contem-oraneous +2 lags	MA of 2 Lags	MA of Contem-poraneous +4 lags	MA of Contem-poraneous +8 lags
Crisis elsewhere	**7.45 (3.8)**	**8.33 (4.0)**	**8.14 (4.3)**	**8.72 (4.0)**	**8.83 (3.8)**
Capital controls	−1.66 (0.7)	0.22 (0.1)	0.66 (0.3)	0.48 (0.2)	1.24 (0.4)
Government victory	−4.24 (1.0)	−1.71 (0.3)	−0.60 (0.2)	5.30 (1.6)	−0.45 (0.2)
Government loss	−3.45 (0.9)	−7.44 (1.3)	−3.34 (1.2)	2.49 (0.8)	−0.63 (0.2)
Credit growth	0.19 (1.8)	0.11 (0.8)	0.10 (1.2)	−0.00 (0.0)	−0.09 (0.4)
Inflation rate	**0.75 (3.5)**	**0.57 (2.4)**	0.40 (1.9)	**0.59 (2.1)**	0.64 (1.8)
Output growth	0.21 (0.6)	−0.39 (0.9)	−0.50 (1.4)	−0.74 (1.3)	−0.36 (0.4)
Employment growth	0.37 (0.7)	0.86 (1.5)	0.78 (1.5)	1.08 (1.6)	1.30 (1.6)
Unemploy-ment rate	**0.86 (3.0)**	**0.96 (3.2)**	**0.92 (3.5)**	**1.04 (3.3)**	**1.19 (3.4)**
Budget position/GDP	0.47 (1.9)	0.41 (1.6)	0.35 (1.5)	0.46 (1.6)	0.57 (1.8)
Current account/GDP	−0.23 (0.8)	−0.36 (1.1)	−0.51 (1.9)	−0.42 (1.2)	−0.34 (0.8)
Number of observations	645	626	703	608	572
McFadden's R^2	0.15	0.12	0.13	0.12	0.10
Joint test for slopes of χ^2 (11)	**55**	**46**	**53**	**43**	**36**

Notes: Probit slope derivatives (× 100, to convert into percentages) and associated z-statistics (for hypothesis of no effect). Model estimated with a constant, by maximum likelihood. Slopes significantly different from zero at the 0.05 value are in bold.

contagion coefficient for the EMS subsample and the fact that "events" matter as much as crises point to the operation of the competitiveness channel modeled by Gerlach and Smets (1995) and Andersen (1994). But these results are also compatible with theories that emphasize the information-coordination effect of exchange market events.

We performed a number of further robustness checks that are not reported here. These include adding a lagged contagion term, which represents the incidence of a currency crisis (in a different country) in the preceding quarter (as opposed to contemporaneously); adding cross products of the contagion term and the remaining regressors; adding

Table 2. *Sensitivity analysis*

	2 Quarter Window, 2σ Threshold	Increased Weight on Exchange Rates	Pre-1979	EMS	Only Immobile Capital	With Contemporaneous Events
Crisis elsewhere	**9.38 (3.5)**	**7.42 (3.3)**	**12.31 (2.8)**	**19.90 (3.4)**	**7.88 (2.9)**	**6.99 (3.4)**
Capital controls	2.43 (1.1)	−0.50 (0.2)	5.41 (0.8)	**10.05 (2.0)**	N/A	0.18 (0.1)
Government victory	**5.67 (2.0)**	4.48 (0.9)	−9.52 (0.8)	2.22 (0.3)	−1.64 (0.2)	−1.13 (0.2)
Government loss	−1.74 (0.4)	−1.90 (0.3)	−14.57 (1.2)	−1.57 (0.3)	−4.71 (0.7)	−6.60 (1.2)
Credit growth	0.09 (0.8)	0.09 (0.6)	0.34 (1.3)	0.13 (0.7)	0.22 (1.2)	0.14 (1.0)
Inflation rate	0.26 (1.4)	0.47 (1.7)	0.17 (0.4)	0.01 (0.0)	**0.59 (2.0)**	**0.58 (2.4)**
Output growth	0.19 (0.8)	−0.07 (0.1)	−0.97 (1.1)	−0.70 (0.9)	−0.68 (1.2)	−0.40 (0.9)
Employment growth	**1.27 (2.6)**	0.52 (0.8)	−0.12 (0.1)	1.51 (1.1)	0.37 (0.5)	0.87 (1.5)
Unemployment rate	0.19 (0.8)	0.45 (1.4)	**4.06 (3.0)**	1.44 (1.7)	**0.91 (2.4)**	**0.99 (3.2)**
Budget position/ GDP	0.05 (0.3)	0.47 (1.7)	1.16 (1.6)	−0.10 (0.3)	0.38 (1.1)	0.40 (1.5)
Current account/ GDP	−0.47 (1.9)	**−0.89 (2.6)**	−1.48 (1.7)	0.08 (0.2)	−0.23 (0.5)	−0.36 (1.1)
Number of observations	326	623	233	224	425	626
McFadden's R^2	0.32	0.09	0.17	0.21	0.11	0.12
Joint test for slopes χ^2 (11)	55	36	31	28	28	45

Notes: Probit slope derivatives ($\times 100$, to convert into percentages) and associated z-statistics (for hypothesis of no effect). Model estimated with a constant, by maximum likelihood. Slopes significantly different from zero at the 0.05 value are in bold. All regressors are expressed as equally weighted moving averages of contemporaneous and two quarterly lags.

money growth, long interest rates, wages, exports and imports to the standard set of explanatory variables; using Huber-White covariance estimators instead of standard ones; and separating out the effects of contemporaneous and lagged regressors. Again, none of these tests disturbs our central finding that speculative attacks in other countries significantly increase the odds of a currency crisis.[20]

V. Conclusion

We have reviewed the theoretical and empirical literatures on crises in foreign exchange markets with an eye toward the prevalence of contagion. While the possibility of contagious currency crises is a pressing policy issue, the debate surrounding it points up the limitations of existing research. The literature is replete with theoretical models highlighting the motives for and dynamics of speculative attacks on pegged currencies and potential channels of contagion, but empirical work has lagged behind. Stories of contagion abound, but systematic empirical analysis is lacking.

Here we have taken a first step toward such an analysis. A battery of empirical specifications fails to reject, at high levels of significance, the hypothesis of contagion. Our central finding is that a speculative attack elsewhere in the world increases the odds of an attack on the domestic currency by eight percent.

A limitation of our approach is the difficulty of distinguishing the effects of crises in neighboring countries (contagion *per se*) and from the effects of global shocks (unobserved environmental factors). This situation is familiar to epidemiologists, for whom the problem is one of determining whether the spread of a virus reflects the contagious nature of the germ or the disease-conducive nature of the environment. The strategy adopted there has been to place additional structure on the problem. In future work we plan to adopt a similar approach, asking for example whether countries with close commercial and macroeconomic ties are particularly susceptible to contagion. We plan to weight our measure of currency crises in neighboring countries by measures of the economic proximity of neighbors (for example, by the share of the two countries' trade which they conduct with one another, or by the similarity of their monetary and fiscal policies). This

---

[20] One of the few indications of sensitivity stems from the inclusion of year-specific controls; this results in point estimates of ω of around 4 percent, and correspondingly marginally statistical evidence against the hypothesis H_0: $\omega = 0$. Since contagion would result in the clustering of speculative attacks over time which could be well picked up by time-specific fixed effects, it is hard to interpret this result. Also, controlling for the IMF's real effective exchange rate (computed using relative normalized unit-value costs) reduces both the sample size (since the series is only available from 1975) and the magnitude of ω by around a half. The estimate of ω falls to around four percent and is of more marginal statistical significance.

approach would better distinguish contagion *per se* from the effects of common unobservable shocks. It would better identify the channels through which contagious currency crises are transmitted.

References

Andersen, Torben: Shocks and the viability of a fixed exchange rate commitment. CEPR DP 969, 1994.

Bensaid, Bernard and Jeanne, Olivier: The instability of fixed exchange rate systems when raising the nominal interest rate is costly. Unpublished manuscript, ENPC-CERAS, Paris, 1993.

Barro, Robert and Gordon, David: Rules, discretion and reputation in a model of monetary policy. *Journal of Monetary Economics 12*, 101–22, 1983.

Blackburn, Keith and Sola, Mario: Speculative currency attacks and balance of payments crises. *Journal of Economic Surveys 7*, 119–44, 1993.

Buiter, Willem, Corsetti, Giancarlo and Pesenti, Paolo: *Financial Markets and International Monetary Cooperation*, Cambridge University Press, Cambridge, 1996.

Burki, Shahid and Edwards, Sebastian: Latin America after Mexico: Quickening the pace. Unpublished manuscript, World Bank, 1995.

Calvo, Guillermo: Varieties of capital-market crises. Unpublished manuscript, University of Maryland, 1995.

Calvo, Guillermo A.: Capital flows and macroeconomic management: Tequila lessons. Unpublished manuscript, University of Maryland, 1996.

Calvo, Sara and Reinhart, Carmen: Capital inflows to Latin America: Is there evidence of contagion effects. Unpublished manuscript, World Bank and International Monetary Fund, 1995.

Caplin, Andrew and Leahy, John: Business as usual, market crashes, and wisdom after the fact. *American Economic Review 84*, 548–65, 1994.

De Kock, Gabriel and Grilli, Vittorio: Fiscal policies and the choice of exchange rate regime. *Economic Journal 103*, 347–56, 1993.

Diamond, Douglas and Dibvig, Phillip: Bank runs, deposit insurance, and liquidity. *Journal of Political Economy 91*, 401–19, 1983.

Dornbusch, Rudiger, Goldfajn, Ilan and Valdés, Rodrigo: Currency crises and collapses. *Brookings Papers on Economic Activity 2*, 219–95, 1995.

Drazen, Allan and Masson, Paul R.: Credibility of policies versus credibility of policymakers. *Quarterly Journal of Economics CIX*, 735–54, 1994.

Edwards, Sebastian: *Real Exchange Rates, Devaluation, and Adjustment: Exchange Rate Policies in Developing Countries*, MIT Press, Cambridge, MA, 1989.

Eichengreen, Barry, Rose, Andrew K. and Wyplosz, Charles: Exchange market mayhem: The antecedents and aftermath of speculative attacks. *Economic Policy 21*, 249–312, 1995.

Eichengreen, Barry, Rose Andrew K. and Wyplosz, Charles: Speculative attacks on pegged exchange rates: An empirical exploration with special reference to the European monetary system. Forthcoming in Matthew Canzoneri, Paul Masson and Vittorio Grilli (eds.), *The New Trans-Atlantic Economy*, Cambridge University Press, Cambridge, 1996.

Flood, Robert and Garber, Peter: Collapsing exchange rate regimes: Some linear examples. *Journal of International Economics 17*, 1–13, 1984.

Froot, Kenneth and Rogoff, Kenneth: Perspectives on PPP and long-term real exchange rates. In Gene Grossman and Kenneth Rogoff (eds.), *Handbook of International Economics 3*, North-Holland, Amsterdam, 1647–88, 1995.

Frankel, Jeffrey A. and Rose, Andrew K.: An empirical characterization of nominal exchange rates. In Gene Grossman and Kenneth Rogoff (eds.), *Handbook of International Economics 3*, North Holland, Amsterdam, 1689–1729, 1995.

Gerlach, Stefan and Smets, Frank: Contagious speculative attacks. *European Journal of Political Economy 11*, 5–63, 1995.

Girton, Lance and Roper, Don: A monetary model of exchange market pressure applied to postwar Canadian experience. *American Economic Review 67*, 537–48, 1977.

Goldfajn, Ilan and Valdés, Rodrigo: Balance of payments crises and capital flows: The role of liquidity. Unpublished manuscript, MIT, 1995.

Grilli, Vittorio: Buying and selling attacks on fixed exchange rate systems. *Journal of International Economics 20*, 143–56, 1986.

International Monetary Fund: *International Capital Markets*, Special Issue, July, 1993.

Jeanne, Olivier: Are currency crises caused by the fundamentals or by self-fulfilling speculation: A test. Unpublished manuscript. ENPC-CERAS, Paris, 1995a.

Jeanne, Olivier: Models of currency crises: A tentative synthesis. Unpublished manuscript, ENPC-CERAS, Paris, 1995b.

Kaminsky, Graciela and Reinhart, Carmen: The twin crises: The causes of banking and balance-of-payments problems. Unpublished manuscript, Federal Reserve Board and International Monetary Fund, 1996.

Krugman, Paul: A model of balance of payments crises. *Journal of Money, Credit and Banking 11*, 311–25, 1979.

Krugman, Paul: Are currency crises self-fulfilling? Forthcoming in *NBER Macroeconomics Annual*, 1996.

Moreno, Ramon: Macroeconomic behavior during periods of speculative pressure or realignment: Evidence from Pacific Basin economies. *Economic Review 3*, Federal Reserve Bank of San Francisco, 3–16, 1995.

Murphy, Robert: Stock prices, real exchange rates and optimal capital accumulation. *IMF Staff Papers 36*, 102–28, 1989.

Obstfeld, Maurice: Rational and self-fulfilling balance of payments crises. *American Economic Review 76*, 72–81, 1986.

Obstfeld, Maurice: Destabilizing effects of exchange rate escape clauses. NBER WP 2603, 1991.

Obstfeld, Maurice: The logic of currency crises. *Cahiers économiques et monétaires 43*, 189–213, 1994.

Obstfeld, Maurice: International currency experience: New lessons and lessons relearned. *Brookings Papers on Economic Activity 2*, 119–220, 1995.

Ozkan, Gulcin and Sutherland, Alan: Policy measures to avoid a currency crisis. *Economic Journal 105*, 510–19, 1995.

Schmukler, Sergio and Frankel, Jeffrey: Crisis, contagion and country funds. Unpublished manuscript, University of California, Berkeley, 1996.

Shiller, Robert: Conversation, information, and herd behavior. *American Economic Review Papers and Proceedings 85*, 181–85, 1995.

Valdés, Rodrigo O.: Emerging market contagion: Evidence and theory. Unpublished manuscript, MIT, 1996.

Wyplosz, Charles: Capital controls and balance of payments crises. *Journal of International Money and Finance 5*, 167–80, 1986.

The Credibility of a Fixed Exchange Rate: How Reputation is Gained or Lost*

Steinar Holden

University of Oslo, N-0317 Oslo, Norway

Birger Vikøren

Norges Bank, N-0107 Oslo, Norway

Abstract

We examine the interest rate differential between each of the four largest Nordic countries and the countries of their foreign currency baskets on monthly data for the period 1978/79–92. The interest rate differential is assumed to reflect devaluation expectations, which partly depend on government reputation. We investigate the formation of the reputation of the government, assuming that reputation is updated using Bayes's formula. It is shown theoretically that when there is no devaluation, the improvement in government reputation is larger, the larger the prior devaluation expectations. For Norway, the evidence gives support to this assertion.

I. Introduction

In the 1980s and early 1990s, the Nordic countries, as well as the countries within the EMS, attempted to maintain fixed exchange rates. An important reason for this policy was to achieve credibility for a low inflation target. For many of these countries, however, the high interest rate differential relative to the D-mark/currency basket reflected that the fixed exchange rate regime was not credible. This raises two questions: why were the regimes not credible and, more generally, what determines the credibility of fixed exchange rate regimes?

Questions of this type may be handled within the framework of the

*This is a revised version of Holden and Vikøren (1994b). We have benefited from comments on an earlier version by Sigbjørn Atle Berg, Asbjørn Rødseth, Øistein Røisland, two anonymous referees and participants at seminars at the University of Oslo, the University of Uppsala, Stockholm School of Economics and the European Economic Association in Maastricht, and from discussions with Torben Andersen, Alex Cukierman, Tore Schweder, Lars Svensson and Anders Vredin. Per-Anders Edin has generously provided some of the data. The first author's work is part of the research project "Unemployment, Institutions and Economic Policy" at SNF, Oslo. Financial support from the Research Council of Norway is gratefully acknowledged.

literature on policy credibility. The typical idea in this literature, following Barro and Gordon (1983) and Backus and Driffill (1985), is that the existence of nominal rigidities provides the government with a temptation to inflate the economy, e.g. by devaluing the currency. A surprise devaluation reduces real wages in the short run, thus increasing employment and/ or improving the balance of payments. However, a devaluation also involves costs in the form of higher inflation and loss of credibility, and the government will only devalue if the short-run gain (the temptation) outweighs the costs. The crucial feature in this literature is that different types of governments vary in their emphasis on the costs of higher inflation: "tough" governments give higher priority to keeping inflation low as compared to "weak" governments. Thus, a weak government may choose to devalue in a situation where a tough government would not.

The devaluation expectations in the market thus depend on two terms: (i) the market's perception of the temptation faced by the government and (ii) the market's perception of the type of government, where the latter may be loosely defined as the reputation of the government. In much of the literature the focus has been on the importance of reputation. Typically, it is argued that a government which refrains from devaluing signals that it gives priority to keeping inflation down, and thus improves its reputation. However, in recent work Drazen and Masson (1994) and Masson (1995) emphasise that maintaining a fixed exchange rate may also have an opposing effect: if maintaining a fixed exchange rate has adverse effects on unemployment, the temptation to devalue may be increased. In certain situations, this latter effect may dominate, in which case maintaining a fixed exchange rate could lead to stronger devaluation expectations.

In this paper we attempt to investigate the determination of the interest rate differential between each of the four largest Nordic countries and the countries of their currency baskets, for the period 1978/79–92, based on a theoretical model of policy credibility. The analysis serves two purposes. First, it clarifies the evolution of the credibility of the recent fixed exchange rate regimes in the Nordic countries. This aspect is related to work by Rose and Svensson (1991, 1993), Lindberg et al. (1991) and Chen and Giovannini (1993), who have attempted to explain interest rate differentials by macroeconomic variables that may affect devaluation expectations.

Second, we provide empirical evidence regarding the possible importance of reputation effects. In previous work on this issue, Andersen and Risager (1988) argue that the decline in Danish interest rates after 1982 was due to improved credibility of exchange rate policy. We take the empirical analysis one step further by attempting to distinguish the temptation to devalue from reputation. Without a distinction between the effect of reputation and the effect of temptation, it seems very hard to assess the empirical importance of reputation effects. In view of the vast attention the concept of reputation has received in both the literature and the economic policy debate, this seems to be a highly important issue.

To capture empirically the effects of reputation, we exploit a feature of Bayes's law. Intuitively, the reputation of the government improves as long as it does not devalue. However, under Bayesian updating we can be more precise; the improvement in reputation is greater, the higher the prior devaluation expectations. At the other extreme, if the market has expected — with high probability — that no devaluation will take place, the observation that no devaluation has occurred does not provide any further information and will not improve reputation. As devaluation expectations are reflected in the interest rate differential, the improvement in reputation if there is no devaluation should be greater, the larger the prior interest rate differential.

The paper is organised as follows. In Section II we present the theoretical model. This model serves as a theoretical framework for the formation of devaluation expectations, with special emphasis on how government reputation evolves over time. The empirical results are in Section III, while some concluding remarks are given in Section IV.

II. A Theoretical Framework

The basic model is a two-period, open-economy Barro and Gordon (1983) model, almost identical to the one used by Drazen and Masson (1994). The economy is completely open, and for simplicity the price level is set equal to the exchange rate. Thus the rate of inflation is $\pi_t = e_t - e_{t-1}$, where e_t is the log of the exchange rate (measured in units of domestic currency per unit of a basket of foreign currencies at the end of month t). Surprise inflation equals the rate of devaluation in excess of the expected rate of devaluation,

$$\pi_t - \pi_t^{\mathrm{E}} = e_t - e_{t-1} - (\mathrm{E}_{t-1}e_t - e_{t-1}) = e_t - \mathrm{E}_{t-1}e_t, \tag{1}$$

where E_{t-1} is the expectation operator, conditional on information up to period $t-1$.

As in the original Barro–Gordon model, the existence of nominal rigidities is assumed to cause a short-run gain from surprise inflation. We specify this relationship by assuming that surprise inflation reduces unemployment u_t relative to the natural rate u_N. The rate of unemployment is also assumed to be affected by its lagged value:

$$u_t = u_N - \sqrt{a}\,[(\pi_t - \pi_t^{\mathrm{E}}) - \delta(u_{t-1} - u_N)] \qquad a > 0,\ \delta > 0. \tag{2}$$

As will become apparent below, persistence in the rate of unemployment implies that the gain from surprise inflation depends on the lagged rate of unemployment.

The government's objective is to minimize an expected discounted loss function, where each period's loss is quadratic in the deviation of unemployment from a target level below the natural rate, $u_N - K$ (where $K > 0$ captures distortions that cause the natural rate to exceed the optimal), as well as in actual inflation. There are two different types of governments, tough (T) and weak (W), which differ in their evaluation of the costs of inflation. The market does not know which type the government is. The intertemporal loss function of a government of type i, conditioned on information available at $t = 1$, is

$$\Lambda^i = L_1^i + \beta E_1 L_2^i = (u_1 - u_N + \eta_1 + K)^2 + \theta^i (\pi_1)^2$$
$$+ \beta E_1 [(u_2 - u_N + \eta_2 + K)^2 + \theta^i (\pi_2)^2 \qquad i = T, W. \qquad (3)$$

β is the discount factor, and $\theta^T > \theta^W > 0$ reflects that the tough government attaches more weight to inflation in its objective function. η_t is a stochastic shock, which is unobservable to the market. η_t captures the difference between the information sets of the government and the market; see Cukierman (1992) for an interesting discussion of such informational differences. First, the market does not have exact knowledge about the preferences of the government. Second, the government may know more about the economic situation than the market does. Third, in reality, the economic situation is much more complex than the present model suggests, and the market does not know how the government evaluates the economic situation. For simplicity, η_1 and η_2 are assumed to be independent.[1]

We follow Drazen and Masson and restrict consideration to two policy alternatives for the government in each period: keeping the exchange rate fixed or devaluing by an exogenously given rate s. This restriction has the advantage that for small shocks, a devaluation of fixed size entails inflation which is too high, so that it is better to keep the exchange rate fixed. Without this restriction, the fact that the game ends in period 2 (thus there are no reputation effects in that period) would imply that devaluing dominates maintaining a fixed parity in period 2 regardless of the size of the shock.[2]

---

[1] Drazen and Masson include the stochastic term in the equation for the rate of unemployment, and not in the preferences of government, but the resulting model is almost identical.

[2] The same results could also be obtained in a model where the size of the devaluation is chosen optimally. However, this would require introducing an explicit cost of a devaluation in period 2, to capture the future loss of reputation.

The main issue of interest in our analysis is the formation of devaluation expectations. The probability of a devaluation in period t (as seen by the market), denoted μ_t, can be written as

$$\mu_t = p_t \rho_t^W + (1 - p_t) \rho_t^T, \tag{4}$$

where p_t is the probability in period t that the government is of type W, and ρ_t^i is the probability that a government of type i will devalue, $i = W$ or T. We define the reputation of the government as the probability that it is tough, $1 - p_t$. The reputation of the government in period 1, $1 - p_1$, is exogenous ($0 < p_1 < 1$); we focus on how $1 - p_2$ depends on the observable variables in period 1. If the market observes an action D (devaluation) in period 1, and updates the probability according to Bayes's law, p_2 is given by

$$p_2(D) \equiv \Pr(\text{weak}|D) = \frac{\Pr(D|\text{weak})}{\Pr(D)} \Pr(\text{weak}) \tag{5}$$

or

$$p_2(D) = \frac{\rho_1^W}{p_1 \rho_1^W + (1 - p_1) \rho_1^T} p_1. \tag{6}$$

Correspondingly, if no devaluation takes place in period 1 (fixed exchange rate F), p_2 is given by

$$p_2(F) = \frac{1 - \rho_1^W}{p_1(1 - \rho_1^W) + (1 - p_1)(1 - \rho_1^T)} p_1. \tag{7}$$

To solve the model, we start with the government decision problem in period 2 to derive ρ_2^W and ρ_2^T. As will become clear below, ρ_2^W and ρ_2^T depend on μ_2, which again depends on p_2 and thus also on ρ_1^W and ρ_1^T. Hence, these variables must be solved for simultaneously.

Let $L_2^{iD}(j)$ denote the single-period loss of a type i government that devalues in the second period (where j was the first period action). The government will devalue in period 2 if $L_2^{iD}(j) - L_2^{iF}(j) < 0$, or, using (1)–(3) and rearranging, if

$$-as + 2a[\mu_2(j)s + \varepsilon_2 + \kappa + \delta(u_1(j) - u_N)] > \theta^i s,$$

$$\text{where } \kappa = K/\sqrt{a} \quad \text{and} \quad \varepsilon_t = \eta_t/\sqrt{a}. \tag{8}$$

The l.h.s. of (8) measures the gain from increased output (the temptation), whereas the r.h.s. shows the associated costs due to higher inflation. Note that the lagged rate of unemployment has a direct positive effect on the temptation. This reflects that the marginal loss of unemployment (i.e., the gain from a reduction in unemployment) is increasing in the rate of unemployment.

Equality in (8) defines a critical value of the shock ε_2:

$$\hat{\varepsilon}_2^i(j) = \frac{(a+\theta^i)s}{2a} - \kappa - \mu_2(j)s - \delta(u_1(j) - u_N).\tag{9}$$

If the realization of ε_t is below the critical value, a policy of maintaining the fixed parity is optimal; if it is above, a devaluation is optimal. It follows from $\theta^T > \theta^W$ that $\hat{\varepsilon}_2^T(j) > \hat{\varepsilon}_2^W(j)$; a tough government is less inclined to devalue. The distribution of ε_t is assumed to be uniform between $-v$ and v, so that

$$\rho_2^i(j) = \Pr(\varepsilon_2 > \hat{\varepsilon}_2^i(j)) = \frac{v - \hat{\varepsilon}_2^i(j)}{2v},\tag{10}$$

as long as $\varepsilon_t \in [-v, v]$ (for ε_t outside this interval, ρ_2^i is equal to 0 ($\varepsilon_t < -v$) or 1 ($\varepsilon_t > v$)).

The period 1 decision problem for a government of type i provides a critical value $\hat{\varepsilon}_1^i$ such that $\Lambda^i(D) = \Lambda^i(F)$, where Λ^i is given by (3). A government of type i devalues if and only if $\varepsilon_1 > \hat{\varepsilon}_1^i$, where

$$\hat{\varepsilon}_1^i = \frac{(a+\theta^i)s}{2a} - \mu_1 s - \kappa - \delta(u_0 - u_N) + \frac{\beta}{2as}[E_1 L_2^i(D) - E_1 L_2^i(F)].\tag{11}$$

The complete model consists of 21 equations (some non-linear) that must be solved simultaneously. These equations are with associated endogenous variable in parentheses, where $j = D$, F, $i = W$, T: (2) ($u_1(j)$), (4) (μ_1, $\mu_2(j)$), (6) ($p_2(D)$), (7) $p_2(F)$), (9) ($\hat{\varepsilon}_2^i(j)$), (10) ($\rho_2^i(j)$), (11) ($\hat{\varepsilon}_1^i$), two equations of the same type as (10) (ρ_1^i), and two equations for $E_1 L_2^i(D) - E_1 L_2^i(F)$. Some substitutions and simplifications are possible, but the complexity of the model implies that it has to be solved numerically.[3]

Prior to presenting the numerical results, we consider the devaluation expectations in the market, given by the probability that a devaluation will occur, μ_t. As seen from (4), this probability depends on (a) the probabilities that a government of a certain type will devalue (ρ_t^i) (which depend on the temptation to devalue), and (b) the reputation of the government (p_t). If the government devalues in period 1, this has two effects on the probability of devaluation in period 2. First, the devaluation affects the temptation to

---

[3] Theoretically, we cannot rule out multiple equilibria. To explore this possibility, we simulated the model with the initial values of the endogenous variables drawn randomly; when the model converges, it always converges to the same solution (barring numerical inaccuracy).

devalue through a reduction in the unemployment rate. Second, the devaluation affects the reputation of the government. As for the latter effect, it is readily seen from (6) and (7) that $1-p_2(F)>1-p_1>1-p_2(D)$ (it is easy to show that a weak government is more likely to devalue than a tough, so that $\rho_1^W>\rho_1^T$). The reputation of the government deteriorates if there is a devaluation, while it improves if the government maintains a fixed parity.

Drazen and Masson (1994) analyse how the devaluation expectations in period 2 depend on whether a devaluation takes place in period 1. They show that keeping a fixed parity may have such a strong positive impact on the temptation to devalue, through an increase in the unemployment rate, that this dominates the positive effect on reputation. Thus, maintaining a fixed parity may actually lead to higher devaluation expectations. (This result is also brought out in Table 1 below).

In contrast, we try to distinguish empirically between the effect of reputation and the effect of temptation. More precisely, we attempt to investigate how the improvement in reputation if there is no devaluation depends on the devaluation expectations in period 1. To do this, note that (7) can be rewritten as

$$1-p_2(F)=\frac{(1-p_1)k}{p_1+(1-p_1)k} \quad \text{where} \quad k=\frac{1-\rho_1^T}{1-\rho_1^W}. \tag{12}$$

k is the probability that a strong government will maintain fixed parity relative to the probability that a weak government will maintain fixed parity. $1-p_2(F)$ is increasing in k, so the improvement in reputation if no devaluation takes place is greater, the higher k is. In order to find how k depends on the devaluation expectations, we differentiate k with respect to one of the exogenous variables, u_0, and obtain

$$\frac{dk}{du_0}=\frac{1-\rho_1^T}{1-\rho_1^W}\left(\frac{d\rho_1^W/du_0}{1-\rho_1^W}-\frac{d\rho_1^T/du_0}{1-\rho_1^T}\right). \tag{13}$$

It follows that $dk/du_0>0$ if and only if

$$\frac{d\rho_1^W/du_0}{1-\rho_1^W}-\frac{d\rho_1^T/du_0}{1-\rho_1^T}>0. \tag{14}$$

The relationship between ρ_1^i and u_0 is complex, but the numerical simulations reported in Table 1 indicate that (14) holds, so $1-p_2(F)$ is increasing in u_0. (This relationship appears robust, as it does not seem to rely on specific parameter values.) The intuition here is as follows. A rise in unemployment u_0 raises the temptation to devalue for both weak and tough governments, and ρ_1^W and ρ_1^T increase (as seen from (8), lagged unemployment has a positive direct effect on temptation). But as $1-\rho_1^W < 1-\rho_1^T$, the probability that a weak government maintains fixed parity is reduced relatively more, so that the increase in k and $1-p_2(F)$ when no devaluation takes place is larger, the greater u_0 is. The issue of devaluation may be viewed as a "test", and a government that does not devalue "passes the test". The higher u_0 is, the greater the temptation to devalue, the higher the prior devaluation expectations, and the more powerful the test. The amount of information provided by the test increases with its powerfulness; hence the improvement in reputation is greater, the higher u_0 is. The result from the simulations that will be exploited in the empirical investigation in Section III is that the improvement in reputation is greater, the higher the prior devaluation expectations; $1-p_2(F)$ is increasing in μ_1 (see Table 1).

An implicit assumption in the theoretical model is that it is always the government that decides whether to devalue. This assumption is standard in the credibility literature; indeed, the concept of reputation is hardly meaningful if the government cannot choose whether to devalue. Yet the experience in the Nordic countries in 1992, when the Finnish, Swedish and Norwegian currencies were floated, suggests on the contrary that speculative forces are a dominant element. A more realistic model would allow for both government decisions and speculative attacks. In such a model, devaluation expectations would depend on both the probability that the government chooses to devalue and the probability that a successful speculative attack occurs. Clearly, learning effects of the type captured by our reputation variables will influence the market's expectations regarding a devaluation chosen by the government. Thus, our reputation variables do not require that devaluations always take place due to a government decision, only that a devaluation may be chosen by the government. This is clearly

Table 1. *Effects of the rate of unemployment u_0 using numerical simulations in GAUSS*

u_0	ρ_1^W	ρ_1^T	μ_1	$p_2(D)$	$p_2(F)$	$\mu_2(D)$	$\mu_2(F)$
0.04	0.0464	0.0014	0.0239	0.9701	0.4885	0.0015	0.0421
0.06	0.2615	0.0220	0.1418	0.9223	0.4302	0.0042	0.0932
0.08	0.5620	0.3179	0.4400	0.6387	0.3910	0.0719	0.1172

Note: The table illustrates that the reputation of the government in period 2, if no devaluation takes place in period 1, is better the higher the prior probability of devaluation (that is, $1-p_2(F)$ is increasing in μ_1). The following parameter values are imposed: $p_1 = 0.5$, $\kappa = 0.02$, $s = 0.1$, $a = 0.25$, $v = 0.15$, $\beta = 0.95$, $\theta^T = 1$, $\theta^W = 0.5$, $\delta = 1.6$, $u_N = 0.04$. We use the same parameter values as Drazen and Masson (1994).

consistent with the Nordic experience, as most of the devaluations in the Nordic countries before 1992 are probably best characterised as chosen by the government (with or without a prior speculative wave) and not caused entirely by speculators.

Within a model which allows for speculative forces, a high interest rate differential may be an indication of the beginning of a speculative wave, and thus lead to increased devaluation expectations. This could give rise to a positive autocorrelation of interest rate differentials.

III. Empirical Specification and Results

The empirical investigation of government reputation requires a measure of the devaluation expectations in the market. Under uncovered interest parity (UIP), the interest rate differential between two currencies is equal to the expected change in the bilateral exchange rate. Formally,

$$i_t - i_t^* = E_t[\Delta e_{t+1}], \tag{15}$$

where $i_t - i_t^*$ is the one-month interest rate differential between investments in domestic and foreign currencies at the end of month t, $\Delta e_{t+1} \equiv e_{t+1} - e_t$, and e_t is the log of the spot exchange rate. More generally, the interest rate differential may reflect a risk premium in addition to the expected change in the exchange rate. Svensson (1992) argues, however, that in target zone regimes with a moderate devaluation risk (like the Nordic countries), the risk premium is likely to be very small. We follow Rose and Svensson (1993) and Chen and Giovannini (1993) and make no explicit allowance for the risk premium in the subsequent analysis.[4]

Figure 1 displays the exchange rates for Denmark, Finland, Norway and Sweden. The data periods begin when the Nordic countries adopted new fixed exchange rate regimes (target zone regimes) in the late 1970s (Denmark became a member of the EMS, while Finland, Norway and Sweden chose unilateral currency basket systems), and end in 1992 when

---

[4] Note that with a fixed exchange rate, the following fairly weak assumptions are sufficient for the interest rate differential to be monotonically increasing in the true devaluation expectations, even if there is a non-negligible risk premium which depends on the variance of the exchange rate: (1) the probability of either a devaluation or a revaluation is always equal to zero, (2) the expected devaluation (revaluation) size is increasing in the devaluation (revaluation) probability. Under these assumptions, the variance of the exchange rate is monotonically increasing in the expected rate of devaluation (or revaluation). To capture the effect of devaluation expectations on the improvement of reputation, the interest rate differential can be used as a measure of devaluation expectations as long as it is monotonically increasing in devaluation expectations, even if it is not equal to them.

Finland, Norway and Sweden let their currencies float.[5] In the period examined, there were in total 18 devaluations of the currencies in our study, and the Finnish marrka was revalued three times; see Edin and Vredin (1993) for a further description of devaluations in the Nordic countries.

Our main interest is the expected change in the central parity, so we

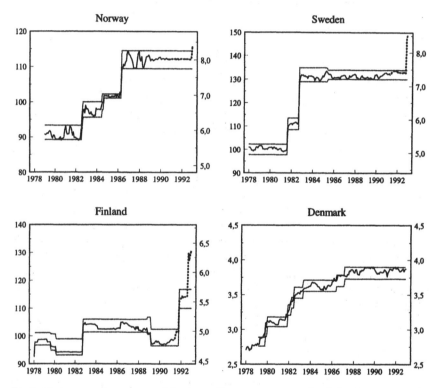

Fig. 1. Exchange rates measured in domestic currency per unit of foreign currency in Denmark, Finland, Norway and Sweden.
Note: Horizontal lines show the upper and lower bounds; dotted lines show the ecu index for Finland, Norway and Sweden, measured at the right axis.

---

[5] We follow Edin and Vredin (1993) and use the Danish krone/D-mark rate for Denmark and the official currency basket indexes for Finland, Norway and Sweden, i.e., a basket of currencies until Norway (October 1990) and Finland and Sweden (early 1991) linked their currencies to the ecu; the ecu index afterwards. As a measure of the interest rate differentials, we use the forward discount that corresponds to the exchange rate applied for each country. The forward discount corresponds to the interest rate differentials in the Euromarket. See the Appendix for sources, and Holden and Vikøren (1994a) for further details.

adjust for the expected movement within the target zone using the drift-adjustment method of Rose and Svensson (1991). Formally, let $e_t \equiv c_t + x_t$, where c_t is the log of the central parity and x_t is the log of the deviation of the exchange rate from the central parity (the exchange rate within the band). Within the drift-adjustment period, the expected rate of devaluation dev_t is defined as

$$dev_t \equiv (i_t - i_t^*) - E_t[\Delta x_{t+1} : NR], \qquad (16)$$

where $: NR$ denotes conditional on no realignment. To compute dev_t, it is necessary to estimate the expectations term. As shown by Lindberg et al. (1991), a linear approximation for the exchange rate process within the band is satisfactory,

$$E_t[\Delta x_{t+1} : NR] = a_0 + a_1 x_t, \qquad \text{where } a_1 < 0. \qquad (17)$$

We use the estimations of $E_t[\Delta x_{t+1} : NR]$ based on (17) that are reported in Holden and Vikøren (1994a) to compute dev_t.

The main objective of the empirical analysis is to distinguish between temptation and reputation. In the theoretical analysis, reducing unemployment is the only motivation for a devaluation; thus unemployment is the only variable that affects the temptation to devalue. In the Nordic countries, improving competitiveness and/or the balance of payments were also important factors behind some of the devaluations. Hence, we include the real exchange rate and the trade balance as possible explanatory variables. In addition, we use the inflation differential, as suggested by Rose and Svensson (1993), and foreign reseves (to capture the ability of the central bank to prevent a speculative attack). Including such a broad set of explanatory variables may justifiably be regarded as *ad hoc*. Yet this seems to reflect the diversity of theories in the field, and almost all the related studies referred to in our introduction have also used a similarly broad set of explanatory variables.

The theoretical analysis in Section II suggests that the improvement in reputation if no devaluation takes place is greater, the higher the prior devaluation expectations. In other words, the improvement in reputation from the previous month if no devaluation takes place is increasing in dev_t. If there is no devaluation for several months, reputation improves in each month, depending on the devaluation expectations in that month. Thus, the improvement in reputation over a longer period without devaluations is increasing in the devaluation expectations of each of the preceding months. However, the theoretical model gives no guidance as to the functional form, so we are forced to make a choice. We choose a simple solution: to use the sum of the previous devaluation expectations, i.e., the cumulated expected rate of devaluation since the last devaluation, which is calculated recursively as follows:

$$cum \, (dev)_t = cum \, (dev)_{t-1} + dev_{t-1},$$

$$\qquad\qquad\qquad \text{if there is no devaluation in period } t-1,$$
$$= 0, \qquad\qquad \text{if there is a devaluation in period } t-1.$$

However, this choice involves strong linearity assumptions. Therefore, to allow for a possible non-linear effect of the devaluation expectations in one month, we include the cumulated squares, $cum \, (dev^2)$; to allow for a non-linear effect over time, we include the square of the cumulated rate, $[cum \, (dev)]^2$.[6]

The $cum \, (dev)$ variable is a measure of how much reputation has improved since the last devaluation (or from the start of the sample period). A problem with this variable is that it is set somewhat arbitrarily at zero after a devaluation; in practice, the reputation of the government after a devaluation depends on the circumstances surrounding the devaluation. Yet it seems difficult to take these circumstances into account in a non-arbitrary way.

Introducing an explicit variable to capture the effect of reputation has clear advantages for the interpretation of the empirical results. Drazen and Masson (1994) have no such variable, and in their empirical specification, the sign of the explanatory variables depends on which of the effects, reputation or temptation, dominates; for France, unemployment was found to have a negative effect in the early 1980s (improved reputation dominated), while later in the same decade the coefficient was positive (increased temptation dominated). Careful interpretation is clearly required. In our approach, the reputation variable, $cum \, (dev)$, captures the reputation effect (and should thus have a negative impact), while the sign of the macroeconomic variables should reflect the effect through the temptation to devalue.

Our $cum \, (dev)$ variable is also related to a variable suggested by Chen and Giovannini (1993). They include the number of months since the last devaluation in the interest rate regressions to capture the improvement in reputation. Our variable, $cum \, (dev)$, has the advantage that it allows the improvement in reputation to depend on the prior devaluation expectations.

We use the interest rate differential as the dependent variable in the regressions. This follows an observation by Lindberg et al. (1991); if some of the explanatory variables in the regressions on dev_t are omitted variables in the regressions on $E_t[\Delta x_{t+1} : NR]$, then the interpretation of the regres-

---

[6] We also tried a few other non-linear specifications of $cum \, (dev)$, before choosing the specifications with the better fit.

sion on dev_t becomes unclear. We allow for the mean reversion effect by including the position of the exchange rate within the band as an explanatory variable, treating it as an endogenous variable.

Our explanatory variables are (see the Appendix for definitions and sources): the seasonally adjusted unemployment rate u_t, the real exchange rate rs_t (calculated from a nominal effective exchange rate and a cost indicator of relative normalized unit labour cost in manufacturing), the seasonally adjusted trade balance tb_t, the inflation differential $\pi_t - \pi_t^*$ (the difference in growth rates of the consumer price index over the preceding 12 months for the country compared to its foreign competitors) and foreign exchange reserves fr_t (the ratio of government's foreign exchange reserves to total imports). The time index refers to the month of publication (for example, u_t refers to the unemployment rate in month $t-1$, published in month t). All the macroeconomic variables enter in linear form.

In the theoretical model, the temptation to devalue depends on the current state of the economy. In practice, the temptation clearly also depends on the expected future state of the economy, and possibly also on the cumulated "need" for a devaluation from the past. We have no data for expectations regarding the macroeconomic variables. However, the expectation may be partly captured by the past evolution of the macroeconomic variables. We used the general-to-specific approach, starting out with a quite general specification for each country separately, with all the explanatory variables included, both in lagged levels and in differences over various lags (annual and monthly change). It turned out that the macroeconomic variables entered very similarly for all countries, so little was lost by imposing the same specification for all countries. We tried imposing the same slope coefficient for all countries, but this restriction was always strongly rejected in an F-test.

The design and interpretation of the regressions require an analysis of the order of integration of the variables. For the dependent variable, the interest rate differential, the unit root hypothesis is rejected for Denmark and Sweden, is on the borderline for Finland, but not rejected for Norway. The non-rejection for Norway may be an artifact of the improvement in reputation of the Norwegian government, which has led to a considerable reduction in the interest rate differential over time, even if this does not involve a unit root. We proceed under the presumption that the interest rate differential is stationary for all countries; this presumption is shared with Bernhardsen (1996), and seems consistent with the graphs of the interest rate differential (see Figure 2). For most of the explanatory variables, the stationary tests are inconclusive. Therefore, the significance levels should be interpreted with caution; possible non-stationarity among the independent variables implies that the t-values do not have the standard distribution; see Bernhardsen (1996) for the appropriate significance levels to use in this model.

The cumulated expected rate of devaluation, which is our main interest, cannot be tested using conventional unit root tests because it does not conform to the maintained hypothesis of these tests. The variables constructed on the basis of *cum* (*dev*) have a very special form, as they increase monotonically, being constant when the expected rate of devaluation is zero, with occasional fallbacks to zero. This reflects how reputation evolves over time, increasing monotonically as long as devaluation expectations exist and no devaluation takes place, but with a loss of reputation if a devaluation takes place.

The lagged dependent variable is included in the regressions to capture the effect of omitted explanatory variables that are autocorrelated, and possibly also speculative waves. (When the lagged dependent variable is excluded, the Durbin-Watson statistic generally takes values below unity; in Holden and Vikøren (1994b) we report similar results in regressions excluding the lagged dependent variable.) We used the generalized method of moments (GMM) because this method allows for autocorrelation and heteroscedasticity in the disturbance term.

Table 2 presents the main results. Unemployment is not significant and has the predicted positive effect for only two countries. The annual increase in the real exchange rate has its predicted positive sign in three out of four equations (not for Denmark), all significant at the 5% level. The inflation differential has the predicted positive sign for all countries, but is not significant at the 5% level. The trade balance has the predicted negative sign in three out of four equations, but is not significant. Foreign reserves have the predicted negative sign in only two of the equations, and for these equations the effect is not significant. A possible reason for the non-significance of this variable is that in recent years governments have often borrowed foreign currency for intervention, rather than tapping reserves. This implies that the amount of reserves is not a precise indicator of the government's capacity to intervene. The position of the exchange rate in the band has a positive impact in three of the equations, suggesting that the positive correlation between expectations of a devaluation and position in the band (a positive x means that the exchange rate is close to the weaker limit) dominates the mean reversion effect. Overall, the results regarding the macroeconomic variables are mixed.

For the reputation variable, the total impact (holding the values of the other right-hand side variables constant) is

$$g_t = b_1 \, cum \, (dev)_t + b_2 cum \, (dev^2)_t + b_3 \, [cum \, (dev)_t]^2, \tag{18}$$

where b_i denotes the estimated coefficients (Table 2) of the respective variables. Figure 2 displays the evolvement of the total impact of the reputation variable, g_t, along with the interest rate differential, for each of the four countries. As seen in Figure 2, $cum\,(dev)_t$ has the predicted negative impact for Norway and Denmark, based on significant coefficients for Norway. The numerical importance is considerable for Norway, where g_t reached its maximum of about 7 percentage points in early 1986, and was fairly stable at about 3 percentage points in the period 1989–92. An implication of this result is that if (hypothetically) Norway had devalued the krone in 1990, and neglecting any effect on the other r.h.s. variables,

Table 2. *Regression results; dependent variable* $(i-i^*)_t$ *and estimation method GMM*

	Denmark 79.5–92.12 (T = 164)	Finland 78.3–92.8 (T = 174)	Norway 79.3–92.11 (T = 165)	Sweden 78.3–92.10 (T = 176)
Constant	2.64	0.61	0.83	0.47
	(1.55)	(1.66)	(0.60)	(0.64)
$(i-i^*)_{t-1}$	0.91	0.81	0.17	0.70
	(6.37)	(21.40)	(1.62)	(6.18)
$(i-i^*)_{t-2}$	−0.16	−0.09	0.12	0.02
	(−1.15)	(−2.65)	(1.38)	(0.36)
u_{t-1}	−0.15	−0.10	0.35	0.14
	(−1.18)	(−1.77)	(1.01)	(0.76)
$\pi_t-\pi_t^*$	0.20	0.005	0.20	0.05
	(1.93)	(0.10)	(1.80)	(0.85)
$\Delta_{12}rs_t$	−0.01	0.03	0.19	0.04
	(−0.31)	(2.72)	(2.55)	(2.26)
tb_{t-1}	0.01	−0.04	−0.23	−0.12
	(0.03)	(−2.39)	(−0.81)	(−1.18)
fr_t	−0.04	0.36	0.43	−0.16
	(−0.23)	(5.18)	(2.52)	(−0.96)
x_t	0.02	0.60	−0.39	0.20
	(0.08)	(10.26)	(−1.43)	(1.25)
$cum\,(dev)_t$	−0.01	0.014	−0.15	−0.01
	(−0.42)	(1.16)	(−3.66)	(−0.53)
$cum\,(dev)_t^2$	−0.0004	−0.002	0.009	0.002
	(−0.10)	(−0.86)	(3.74)	(0.79)
$[cum\,(dev)_t]^2$	0.00007	−0.00003	0.0002	0.00002
	(0.69)	(−2.26)	(3.13)	(0.42)
Diagnostics:				
R^2	0.82	0.73	0.51	0.62
$J(q-k)$	11.28	1.27	3.20	4.60
σ	1.26	1.26	3.35	1.14

Notes: The symbols are: unemployment rate u_t, inflation differential $\pi_t-\pi_t^*$, the real exchange rate rs_t, trade balance tb_t, foreign exchange reserves fr_t, the position of the exchange rate within the band x_t. As for dev_t, see equation (16); $cum\,(dev)_t$, see explanation in the text. x_t is treated as an endogenous variable, and the additional instruments are $x_{t-1}, x_{t-2}, tb_t, tb_{t-2}$.
$J(q-k)$ is a test of overidentifying restrictions, where q is the number of instruments applied and k is the number of coefficients. The test statistic is distributed asymptotically as chi-square with $q-k$ degrees of freedom. R^2 is the multiple correlation coefficient; σ is the standard error of the residuals; T is the number of observations; T-values in parentheses.

the effect on the interest rate differential of a loss in reputation due to a devaluation would have been an increase of about 3 percentage points. There are, however, several reasons to treat this figure with caution. First, the estimated equation is, of course, not the true data-generating process, so although the coefficients for *cum (dev)*, are estimated fairly precisely for Norway, there is considerable uncertainty regarding the direct effect of *cum (dev)*,. Second, a devaluation would in general affect the values of the other explanatory variables, which would again influence the interest rate differential. Third, the loss in reputation due to a devaluation would presumably depend on the circumstances under which the devaluation took place, while the estimated equation does not allow for any such dependency.

IV. Concluding Remarks

We have estimated regressions for the interest rate differential between each of the four largest Nordic countries and the countries of their foreign

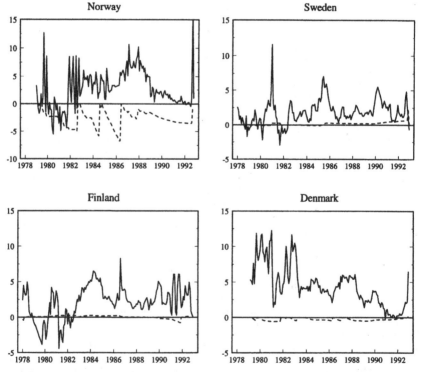

Fig. 2. Interest rate differential as annualized rate (solid line) and the total impact of *cum (dev)*, (broken line).

currency baskets. The interest rate differential, adjusted for the expected movement of the exchange rate within the band, is taken as a measure of devaluation expectations. In line with previous research, e.g. Rose and Svensson (1993), we find that the macroeconomic variables can only to a limited extent explain the variation in the interest rate differentials.

The main focus of the paper, however, is to distinguish the reputation of the government from the temptation to devalue faced by the government. We suggest that the cumulated expected rate of devaluation over the months since the last devaluation ($cum\ (dev)_t$), captures the extent to which the government builds up a reputation by not devaluing when it is expected to. When the cumulated expected rate of devaluation is included in the interest rate regressions, it has the predicted negative impact for Denmark and Norway. For Norway, this variable has a considerable negative impact on the interest rate differential, based on significant coefficients. The point estimate of the effect on the interest rate differential of the loss in reputation due to a hypothetical devaluation in 1990 is about 3 percentage points. Although this figure should be taken with a pinch of salt, it at least illustrates the potential importance of reputation.

Why do the reputation results differ between Norway and the other countries? Regrettably, we do not have any satisfactory explanation, apart from the observation that the significant reputation results for Norway presumably reflect the unique 10 percentage points reduction in the interest rate differential over the period 1988–92.

Given the considerable interest in reputation in both the theoretical literature and the economic policy debate, one might have expected to find stronger effects of reputation than those reported here. However, empirical work on reputation is still in its infancy, and presumably much more work is warranted before a clearer conclusion can be reached: either that reputation is found to be empirically important, or that reputation is a notion of mainly theoretical interest.

Appendix. Data Definitions and Sources

Interest rate differential $(i - i^*)$. For Finland, Norway and Sweden, we used the thirty-day forward discounts on domestic currency vs. either the currency basket index or the ecu index, while for Denmark we used the thirty-day forward discount on the Danish krone vs. the German mark. End-of-month quotations of the forward discounts were used.

Exchange rate within the band (x_t). For Finland, Norway and Sweden, we used the log of the official currency basket indexes and the ecu indexes, while for Denmark we used the log of the krone/D-mark rate. All exchange rates are end-of-month.

Sources (the exchange rate and interest rate differential): Sweden: Sveriges Riksbank and Skandinaviska Enskilda Banken; Finland: Bank of Finland; Norway:

International Financial Statistics (IMF), Skandinaviska Enskilda Banken and Norges Bank; Denmark: *International Financial Statistics* (IMF) and Skandinaviska Enskilda Banken.

The rate of unemployment (u_t) and *trade balance* (tb_t): *Main Economic Indicators* (OECD).

Real exchange rate (rs_t), calculated from a nominal effective exchange rate and a cost indicator of relative normalized unit labour cost in manufacturing; *inflation differential* ($\pi_t - \pi_t^*$), growth rate of the consumer price index over the preceding 12 months (both rs_t and $\pi_t - \pi_t^*$ use weights derived from trade in manufactured goods between industrialized nations); and *foreign exchange reserves* fr_t: *International Financial Statistics* (IMF).

References

Andersen, T. M. and Risager, O.: Stabilization policies, credibility and interest rate determination in a small open economy. *European Economic Review, Papers and Proceedings 32*, 669–79, 1988.

Backus, D. and Driffill, J.: Rational expectations and policy credibility following a change in regime. *Review of Economic Studies 52*, 211–21, 1985.

Barro, R. and Gordon, D.: Rules, discretion, and reputation in a model of monetary policy. *Journal of Monetary Economics 12*, 101–21, 1983.

Bernhardsen, T.: Devaluation expectations and macroeconomic variables: A critical evaluation of the literature. Mimeo, Norges Bank, Oslo, 1996.

Chen, Z. and Giovannini, A.: The determinants of realignment expectations under the EMS: Some empirical regularities. NBER WP 4291, 1993.

Cukierman, A.: *Central Bank Strategy, Credibility and Independence: Theory and Evidence.* MIT Press, Cambridge, MA, 1992.

Drazen, A. and Masson, P. R.: Credibility of policies versus credibility of policymakers. *Quarterly Journal of Economics CIX*, 735–54, 1994.

Edin, P.-A. and Vredin, A.: Devaluation risk in target zones: Evidence from the Nordic countries. *Economic Journal 103*, 161–75, 1993.

Holden, S. and Vikøren, B.: Interest rates in the Nordic countries: Evidence based on devaluation expectations. *Scandinavian Journal of Economics 96* (1), 15–30, 1994a.

Holden, S. and Vikøren, B.: Interest rate differentials and reputation: Evidence from the Nordic countries. Memorandum no. 8, Department of Economics, University of Oslo, 1994b.

Lindberg. H., Svensson, L. E. O. and Söderlind, P.: Devaluation expectations: The Swedish Krona 1982–1991. NBER WP 3918, 1991.

Masson, P. R.: Gaining and losing ERM credibility: The case of United Kingdom. *Economic Journal 105*, 571–82, 1995.

Rose, A. K. and Svensson, L. E. O.: Expected and predicted realignments: The FF/DM exchange rate during the EMS. IIES Seminar Paper 485, University of Stockholm, 1991.

Rose, A. K. and Svensson, L. E. O.: European exchange rate credibility before the fall. IIES Seminar Paper 542, University of Stockholm, 1993.

Svensson, L. E. O.: The foreign exchange risk premium in a target zone with devaluation risk. *Journal of International Economics 33*, 21–40, 1992.

Would a Tobin Tax have Saved the EMS?

Olivier Jeanne*

Ecole Nationale des Ponts et Chaussées-CERAS, F-75007 Paris, France

Abstract

This paper scrutinizes the claim by Eichengreen, Tobin and Wyplosz (1995) that a small tax on foreign exchange transactions would help to stabilize the European Monetary System. We present a target zone model *à la* Svensson (1994) in which an optimizing government is faced with a trade-off between its foreign exchange and its domestic objectives. The introduction of a Tobin tax is shown to improve the credibility of the peg by relaxing the foreign exchange rate constraint and making it less costly for the government to stay in the fixed exchange rate system. We calibrate the model using data on the French franc in 1991–93, and show that the stabilizing effect of a 0.1% Tobin tax would have been quite sizeable.

I. Introduction

According to most economists, the crisis which shook the European Monetary System (EMS) in 1992–93 resulted from a number of factors, including the German unification shock, the recession in Europe, and rising doubts about the future of the European Monetary Union.[1] Without excluding these factors, some economists also trace the origin of the crisis back to the removal of capital controls in 1990; see Eichengreen and Wyplosz (1993) and Portes (1993). In particular, Eichengreen and Wyplosz (1993) argue that fixed exchange rate systems with adjustable parities are intrinsically unstable in the absence of capital controls because they are vulnerable to self-fulfilling speculation. The reintroduction of capital controls, on the basis of which a new, more stable, EMS could be rebuilt is advocated in Eichengreen, Tobin and Wyplosz (1995). Their main proposal is to establish a tax on foreign exchange transactions. This tax was originally advocated by Tobin (1978) to improve the working of the international monetary system under floating exchange rates.

The proposal to establish a Tobin tax has been criticized on several grounds. While some economists have pointed to its distortion costs, others have questioned the mere feasibility of the Tobin tax.[2] In particular,

---

* This paper benefited from comments by Charles Wyplosz and two anonymous referees. All remaining errors are mine.
[1] A review of possible interpretations of the crisis may be found in Eichengreen and Wyplosz (1993) or Svensson (1994b).
[2] Good summaries of these criticisms may be found in Frankel (1995), Garber and Taylor (1995) and Kenen (1995a, b).

Garber and Taylor (1995) argue that the tax needs to be universal because if it were limited to a group of countries, foreign exchange transactions would simply evade the market where they are taxed towards tax-free markets. On the other hand, Kenen (1995b) discuss some accompanying measures which might make the Tobin tax feasible.

The purpose of this paper is essentially to make some progress on the following question: can a small Tobin tax attain the objective assigned to it by its proponents, i.e., stabilize a fixed exchange rate system? The answer to this question if it turned out to be positive, may constitute an encouragement for further research about the costs and benefits of a Tobin tax, as well as the mechanisms for making it non-evadable.

Our analysis is based on a model of a target zone à la Svensson (1994a). In this model we consider an optimizing government which is faced with a trade-off between a foreign exchange objective and a domestic interest rate objective. The tension between these objectives grows stronger when the foreign interest rate becomes very different from the desired domestic interest rate. The government may then be tempted to evade this tension by realigning the central parity, which generates some devaluation expectations aggravating the original trade-off faced by the government.

We then introduce a Tobin tax into the model, and show that it can stabilize the fixed exchange rate system through two different channels. First, the Tobin tax allows the monetary authorities to insulate (to some extent) domestic monetary policy from external shocks, and in this way increases the range of shocks that the system is able to withstand. The second, more indirect, effect of the tax is to reduce the size of realignment expectations. Market participants revise their realignment expectations downward because they know that the tax makes it less costly for the government to defend the currency.

In order to evaluate the empirical relevance of our analysis, we present a calibration of the model based on the experience of the French franc in 1991–93. This calibration provides us with an interpretation of the French franc crisis which is consistent with the view of most economists. We find that the interest rate level desired by the French government was lower than the German interest rate. This generated realignment expectations which constrained the French monetary authorities to maintain their interest rate above the German level.

We then quantify how a very moderate Tobin tax of 0.1% would have changed the trade-off faced by the French government during the sample period. We find that the tax would have allowed France to keep its interest rate much closer to the desired level. As a result, the expected rate of realignment of the French franc *vis-à-vis* the Deutschemark would have been divided by more than five. Thus, our findings suggest that a small

Tobin tax can have a sizeable stabilizing effect on a fixed exchange rate system.

This paper contributes to a small literature which studies the stabilizing properties of capital controls in fixed exchange rate systems. Some papers study the impact of capital controls on the possibility of speculative runs on the foreign exchange reserves of the central bank; cf. Dellas and Stockman (1993), Park and Sachs (1987) and Wyplosz (1986). Wyplosz (1986) and Parks and Sachs (1987) show that capital controls make speculative attacks more difficult because they prevent domestic residents from running on the reserves. On the other hand, Dellas and Stockman (1993) argue that capital controls can have destabilizing properties. In their model, the threat of capital controls may induce private agents to run on the foreign exchange reserves before controls are introduced, which can generate self-fulfilling speculative attacks.

The analysis presented here is closer in spirit to some recent contributions which focus on the cost of defending the currency by raising the interest rate.[3] Ozkan and Sutherland (1995), for example, present a model in which capital controls are stabilizing for the same reason as in the present paper. Bensaid and Jeanne (1996) study the impact of a Tobin tax in a model where self-fulfilling speculation can arise. We show that capital controls can, under some conditions, remove the possibility of self-fulfilling speculation, which is another way in which they may be stabilizing.

The paper is organized as follows. In Section II, we present a simple target zone model, inspired by Svensson (1994a). Section III then scrutinizes the effect of the introduction of a Tobin tax into this target zone model. Section IV quantifies the stabilizing effect of a small 0.1% Tobin tax in the case of the EMS. Section V concludes by suggesting paths for future research.

II. A Simple Target Zone Model

The target zone model *à la* Svensson (1994a) presented in this section is a good framework for analysing the trade-off between monetary independence and exchange rate stability faced by a government in a target zone. In contrast to continuous time target zone models *à la* Krugman (1991), this model endows the government with an objective function and focuses the analysis on the way the government adjusts the exchange rate and the interest rate to exogenous shocks.

---

[3] These papers belong to the "escape clause" approach to fixed exchange rate systems proposed by Obstfeld (1991). This approach is reviewed in Jeanne (1995).

Assumptions

We consider a government[4] which tries to maintain the exchange rate between the domestic currency and a foreign currency close to a fixed level. We assume that the domestic government minimizes the instantaneous loss function:

$$L_t = q(e_t - c_t)^2 + (i_t - \hat{\imath}_t)^2, \tag{1}$$

where e_t denotes the (log) exchange rate, c_t the (log) central parity, i_t the domestic one-period nominal interest rate, and $\hat{\imath}_t$ the target nominal interest rate. The extent to which a loss function like (1) characterizes the behaviour of a government in a target zone is discussed by Svensson (1994a), who introduced this type of modelling. It is intended to represent in the most simple way the trade-off between exchange rate and interest rate targets with which a government is faced in a target zone.

The variable $\hat{\imath}$ is the desired interest rate, corresponding to the "ideal" monetary policy that the government would implement if it had no foreign exchange objective (i.e., if q was equal to zero). Presumably, the ideal monetary policy depends on domestic economic conditions and the ultimate objective of the domestic government. For example, if the government tries to keep the inflation and unemployment rates down, the ideal stance of monetary policy should depend on the current inflation and unemployment levels. The term $(i_t - \hat{\imath}_t)^2$ then represents the cost in terms of inflation or unemployment of a misaligned monetary policy. This term may also reflect the detrimental effects of high interest rates on the banking sector, or the burden of interest payments on the public debt.

We assume in this section that capital is perfectly mobile internationally (some impediments to the free mobility of capital are considered when we introduce the Tobin tax in Section III). Assuming away the foreign exchange risk premium, the domestic nominal interest rate must then satisfy the uncovered interest parity condition:

$$i_t = i_t^* + n\mathrm{E}_t(e_{t+1} - e_t), \tag{2}$$

where i_t^* denotes the foreign one-period nominal interest rate, and n is the number of periods in one year (which must appear in the interest parity condition because i_t and i_t^* are annually compounded).

The government chooses at each period t the exchange rate e_t. This decision is made in two steps. First, the government decides whether it will

---

[4] The domestic monetary authorities are hereafter called "government", leaving aside the question of the allocation of power between the government and the central bank.

realign or not. If it realigns, the government fixes a new central parity $c_t \neq c_{t-1}$.[5] Second, it decides the (log) deviation of the exchange rate from central parity, i.e., the variable

$$s_t = e_t - c_t, \tag{3}$$

hereafter called the *exchange rate relative to central parity*.

It follows that the expected rate of currency depreciation may be written as the sum of two components, the expected rate of realignment and the expected rate of depreciation relative to central parity:

$$E_t(e_{t+1} - e_t) = E_t(c_{t+1} - c_t) + E_t(s_{t+1} - s_t). \tag{4}$$

Our next assumption relates to the determination of the realignment expectations. We assume that the expected rate of realignment is related to the loss function through:

$$E_t(c_{t+1} - c_t) = A \text{ sgn } (s_t) \sqrt{L_t} \tag{5}$$

where A is a positive constant, and sgn (s_t) is the sign of s_t.

This equation may be interpreted as follows. First, the term sgn (s_t) corresponds to the assumption that the expected direction of the realignment depends on whether the exchange rate is above or below the central parity. When s is positive (negative), the domestic currency is weak (strong), and the market anticipates that the realignment, if it occurs, will be a devaluation (revaluation).

Second, the term $\sqrt{L_t}$ reflects the idea that the expected realignment should be an increasing function of the government's loss. When the cost of maintaining the currency at the current parity increases, realignment becomes more probable and the expected size of the realignment is larger. We adopt a square root specification in order to simplify the algebra: as it will appear in the next section, this specification allows us to characterize the equilibrium in a simple linear form. The logic of our result, however, should remain valid with more general specifications.

The variable $x_t = i_t^* - \hat{\imath}_t$ will turn out to be an important variable of the model. It reflects the degree of misalignment between the desired domestic monetary policy and the foreign one. It may come, for example, from the lack of synchronization between the domestic and foreign business cycles. We do not model the origin of the policy misalignment in this paper. We simply take the variable x as exogenous and assume that it is governed by the following autoregressive process:

$$x_t = \rho x_{t-1} + \varepsilon_t \tag{6}$$

---

[5] The government stays in the fixed exchange rate system when it realigns the central parity. Switching to a floating rate regime is a possibility that we do not consider here.

where ε is i.i.d. normal with variance σ^2, and $\rho \in]0, 1[$. This process implies that the average (long-term) value of x is zero, i.e., on average the desired domestic interest rate is the same as the foreign one. Hence, the fixed exchange rate system is viable in the long term: the pressures to which it is submitted are necessarily transitory.

Policy Determination

We now determine how the government optimally chooses its policy variables as a function of the state of the economy. As the loss function of the government depends on its expected future policy, the optimization problem gives rise to a time consistency problem. It is well known that the solution to this type of problem depends on whether the government can commit itself to a rule or determines its policy in a discretionary way. Since there is no apparent way in which the government can commit to a particular rule, the discretionary solution seems more realistic and relevant, and this is the solution concept to which we restrict our attention in what follows.[6] Namely, we assume that at each period t the government sets s_t so as to minimize the loss function (1), taking the expectations of the foreign exchange market $E_t(s_{t+1})$ and $E_t(c_{t+1}-c_t)$ as given. The following proposition characterizes the form of the optimal policy under these assumptions.

Proposition 1. *If $q > n^2\alpha$, the optimal discretionary policy of the government is unique, and given by:*

$$s_t = \frac{n}{n^2(1-\alpha-\rho)+q}(\hat{\imath}_t^* - \hat{\imath}_t) \tag{7}$$

$$\hat{\imath}_t = \frac{n^2(1-\alpha-\rho)\hat{\imath}_t + q\hat{\imath}_t^*}{n^2(1-\alpha-\rho)+q}. \tag{8}$$

Proof: Plugging equations (2) and (4) into the loss funtion (1), the optimization problem of the government may be written:

$$\min_{s_d} \quad qs_t^2 + (\hat{\imath}_t - \hat{\imath}_t)^2 = qs_t^2 + [x_t + nE_t(c_{t+1}-c_t) + nE_ts_{t+1} - ns_t]^2 \tag{9}$$

---

[6] Svensson (1994a) and Laskar (1994) compare the discretionary solution with the rule in a similar setting.

from which it follows that:

$$qs_t = n(i_t - \hat{i}_t) \tag{10}$$

or:

$$s_t = \frac{n^2}{n^2+q}\left[\frac{x_t}{n} + E_t(c_{t+1}-c_t) + E_t(s_{t+1})\right]. \tag{11}$$

Using equation (10), the value of the loss function may be written as a function of the exchange rate relative to central parity:

$$L_t = q\left(1+\frac{q}{n^2}\right)s_t^2 \tag{12}$$

so that the expected rate of realignment is given by:

$$E_t(c_{t+1}-c_t) = \alpha \, \text{sgn}(s_t)|s_t| = \alpha s_t \tag{13}$$

where $\alpha = A\sqrt{q(1+(q/n^2))}$. Plugging this equation into (11), it appears that the state of the system at date t is summarized by x_t, and that s_t is a function $S(\cdot)$ of the state satisfying:

$$S(x_t) = \frac{n^2}{n^2(1-\alpha)+q}\left(\frac{x_t}{n} + E_t S(x_{t+1})\right). \tag{14}$$

One can then show that if $q > n^2\alpha$, the operator defined by equation (14) is a contraction mapping with modulus $(1-\alpha+q/n^2)^{-1} < 1$, from which it follows that (14) has one unique solution $S(\cdot)$; see Sargent (1987, pp. 340–5).[7] Looking for a linear solution of the type $s_t = \lambda x_t$, it is easy to find equation (7). Equations (10) and (7) then yield (8).   Q.E.D.

Proposition 1 states that the equilibrium of the economy is uniquely defined if the inequality $q > n^2\alpha$ is satisfied. It is possible to show that when this condition is not satisfied, the dynamics of the exchange rate in the target zone may be driven by sunspots. Exploring the role of sunspots in this model, while interesting *per se*, is outside the scope of this paper, and we restrict our discussion to the case $q > n^2\alpha$.

In order to interpret Proposition 1, let us consider first the case when there is no policy misalignment, i.e., the foreign interest rate is equal to the desired one ($i_t^* = \hat{i}_t$). As equations (7) and (8) show, the government can reach its foreign exchange and domestic interest rate objectives

---

[7] The details of the application of the contraction mapping theorem to this setting are available on request.

simultaneously, i.e., set the exchange rate *and* the nominal interest rate at their target levels ($s_t = 0$ and $i_t = i_t^* = \hat{\imath}_t$).

The tension between the foreign exchange and the domestic interest rate objectives begins to surface when the foreign interest rate diverges from the desired level. Let us assume, for example, that the foreign monetary policy becomes more restrictive than the desired one ($i_t^* > \hat{\imath}_t$), which may happen following a rise in the foreign interest rate or a fall in the desired interest rate. According to (7), the optimal reaction of the government is to let part of the pressure bear on the exchange rate, i.e., let the domestic currency depreciate below the central parity. By inducing market participants to expect an appreciation of the currency inside the band, this allows the government to set the domestic interest rate below the foreign one. This is the monetary independence offered by the target zone, as stressed by Svensson (1994a).

The beneficial effect of monetary independence is counterbalanced, however, by devaluation expectations. The depreciation of the currency generates realignment expectations, which puts some pressure on the government to *raise* the domestic interest rate. Which effect dominates depends on the credibility of the central parity. When the realignment expectations are structurally small ($\alpha < 1 - \rho$), the government can adjust the domestic interest rate in the desired direction, i.e.:

$$\hat{\imath}_t < i_t < i_t^*. \tag{15}$$

Conversely, when the realignment expectations are structurally large ($\alpha > 1 - \rho$), one obtains the paradoxical result that the government must adjust the domestic interest rate in the opposite direction of the desired one:

$$\hat{\imath}_t < i_t^* < i_t. \tag{16}$$

III. The Target Zone with a Tobin Tax

We now introduce a Tobin tax of rate τ into the target zone model of the preceding section. We assume that in all foreign exchange transaction involving the domestic and foreign currencies, each trader must pay a tax equal to $\tau\%$ of the amount of the transaction. We want to scrutinize how the introduction of this tax changes the impact of the policy misalignment x on the policy of the government and the realignment expectations.

The effect of the Tobin tax is to drive a wedge in the interest parity condition (2). Let us consider an investor who holds domestic one-period bonds. By converting her domestic bonds into foreign bonds and reverting to domestic currency the next period, she gets the (annually compounded) expected return $i_t^* + n\mathrm{E}_t(e_{t+1} - e_t) - 2n\tau$, which must be lower in equilibrium than the return i_t on domestic bonds. Similarly, foreign bonds will be held in equilibrium only if their expected return i_t^* is higher than $i_t - nE_t(e_{t+1} - e_t) - 2n\tau$. It follows that the interest parity condition is replaced by the double inequality:

$$i_t^* + nE_t(e_{t+1} - e_t) - 2n\tau \le i_t \le i_t^* + nE_t(e_{t+1} - e_t) + 2n\tau. \tag{17}$$

The question that we now want to scrutinize is how the optimal policy of the government is changed when the interest parity constraint (2) is replaced by (17). The following result generalizes Proposition 1 to this case.

Proposition 2. *If $q > n^2\alpha$, the optimal discretionary policy is unique and given by:*

$$s_t = S_\tau(i_t^* - \hat{\imath}_t) \tag{18}$$

$$i_t = \frac{q}{n}S_\tau(i_t^* - \hat{\imath}_t) + \hat{\imath}_t \tag{19}$$

where $S_\tau(\cdot)$ is a function satisfying the following properties:

  (i) $S_\tau(\cdot)$ *is increasing;*
  (ii) $S_\tau(\cdot)$ *is antisymmetric, i.e., $\forall x$, $S_\tau(x) + S_\tau(-x) = 0$;*
  (iii) $\partial |S_\tau| / \partial \tau \le 0$, *i.e.: $\tau' \ge \tau \Rightarrow \forall x$, $|S_{\tau'}(x)| \le |S_\tau(x)|$;*
  (iv) *if $\tau > 0$, $S_\tau(\cdot)$ is equal to zero in an interval centered on 0, i.e.:*

$$\exists \eta > 0, \qquad |x| < \eta \Rightarrow S_\tau(x) = 0. \tag{20}$$

Proof: The problem of the government may now be written:

$$\min_{s_t} \ qs_t^2 + (i_t - \hat{\imath}_t)^2 \tag{21}$$

subject to:

$$x_t + nE_t(c_{t+1} - c_t) + nE_t(s_{t+1}) - ns_t - 2n\tau \le i_t - \hat{\imath}_t$$
$$x_t + nE_t(c_{t+1} - c_t) + nE_t(s_{t+1}) - ns_t + 2n\tau \ge i_t - \hat{\imath}_t.$$

This optimization problem gives rise to three cases. The first case is when neither constraint is binding, and the government sets its loss function at zero by taking $i_t - \hat{\imath}_t = s_t = 0$. This is consistent with the constraints if and only if:

$$-2\tau \le \frac{x_t}{n} + E_t(c_{t+1} - c_t) + E_t(s_{t+1}) \le 2\tau. \tag{22}$$

The second case occurs when $x_t/n + E_t(c_{t+1} - c_t) + E_t(s_{t+1}) \geq 2\tau$. Then the first constraint is binding and the exchange rate relative to central parity is given by:

$$s_t = \frac{n^2}{n^2 + q} \left[\frac{x_t}{n} + E_t(c_{t+1} - c_t) + E_t(s_{t+1}) - 2\tau \right]. \tag{23}$$

The third case occurs when $x_t/n + E_t(c_{t+1} - c_t) + E_t(s_{t+1}) \leq -2\tau$. Then the second constraint is binding and:

$$s_t = \frac{n^2}{n^2 + q} \left[\frac{x_t}{n} + E_t(c_{t+1} - c_t) + E_t(s_{t+1}) + 2\tau \right]. \tag{24}$$

In all cases, equation (10) remains true. For the sake of notational simplicity, we summarize our three cases with the following *formula*:

$$s_t = \frac{1}{1+q} f_{2\tau} [x_t + E_t(c_{t+1} - c_t) + E_t(s_{t+1})] \tag{25}$$

where $f_{2\tau}(\cdot)$ is defined by:

$f_{2\tau}(y) = 0 \qquad$ if $-2\tau \leq y \leq 2\tau$

$f_{2\tau}(y) = y - 2\tau \qquad$ if $2\tau \leq y$

$f_{2\tau}(y) = y + 2\tau \qquad$ if $y \leq -2\tau$.

Let us now express the expected rate of realignment in terms of the other variables. Since (10) still applies, equations (12) and (13) remain true, so that (25) may be rewritten:

$$s_t = \frac{n^2}{n^2 + q} f_{2\tau} \left[\frac{x_t}{n} + \alpha s_t + E_t(s_{t+1}) \right] \tag{26}$$

which implies:

$$s_t = \frac{n^2}{n^2(1-\alpha) + q} f_{2\tau} \left[\frac{x_t}{n} + E_t(s_{t+1}) \right]. \tag{27}$$

It follows that if we write the exchange rate relative to central parity as a function of the state $s_t = S_\tau(x_t)$, function $S_\tau(\cdot)$ must satisfy the functional equation:

$$S_\tau(x) = \frac{n^2}{n^2(1-\alpha) + q} f_{2\tau} \left[\frac{x}{n} + ES_\tau(x') \right] \tag{28}$$

with $x' = \rho x + \varepsilon$.

It is possible to check that if $q > n^2\alpha$, the functional operator defined by this equation is a contraction mapping, which ensures the existence and unicity of $S_\tau(\cdot)$.[8] It is not possible to find an explicit formula for $S_\tau(\cdot)$ when τ is different from zero. However, we know that $S_\tau(\cdot)$ is the limit of the sequence of functions $(S_\tau^{(k)}(\cdot))_{k \geq 0}$ defined by:

$$S_\tau^{(k)}(x) = \frac{n^2}{n^2(1-\alpha)+q} f_{2\tau}\left[\frac{x}{n} + \mathrm{E}S_\tau^{(k-1)}(x')\right] \tag{29}$$

for any initial $S_\tau^{(0)}(\cdot)$; see Sargent (1987, p. 343).

Let us now prove properties (i)–(iv). One proves (i) and (ii) by noting that if $S_\tau^{(0)}(\cdot)$ satisfies them, then by induction it is also true of $S_\tau^{(k)}(\cdot)$ for all k, and of $S_\tau(\cdot)$ by taking the limit. Property (iii) results from the fact that $\tau' \geq \tau \Rightarrow |f_{\tau'}(\cdot)| \leq |f_\tau(\cdot)|$. It follows by induction on (29) that $S_{\tau'}^{(0)}(\cdot) = S_\tau^{(0)}(\cdot) \Rightarrow \forall k, \ |S_{\tau'}^{(k)}(\cdot)| \leq |S_\tau^{(k)}(\cdot)|$ and taking the limit gives (iii). In order to prove (iv), note that the antisymmetry property implies that the function $x \mapsto (x/n) + \mathrm{E}S_\tau(\rho x + \varepsilon)$ is equal to 0 in $x = 0$. By continuity of this function, it then follows that $\exists \eta, \ \forall |x| < \eta, \ |(x/n) + \mathrm{E}S_\tau(\rho x + \varepsilon)| < 2\tau$, which using (28) implies $S_\tau(x) = 0$.   Q.E.D.

Figure 1 shows a typical representation of function $S_\tau(\cdot)$. The Tobin tax generates a "honeymoon" effect similar to that put forward in the target zone literature *à la* Krugman (1991). It should be stressed that this honeymoon effect is not due to the existence of the target zone but to the Tobin tax: in the absence of this tax the relationship between the "fundamental" x and the exchange rate relative to central parity is linear. The tax insulates the exchange rate from the fundamental x, and this effect is larger, the higher the level of the tax rate (point (iii)). Moreover, the insulating effect of the tax is complete in a small interval in the middle of the band (point (iv)). This means that as long as the policy misalignment $|\hat{\imath} - i^*|$ is smaller than a bound η, the government can attain its foreign exchange and domestic objectives simultaneously.

The intuition behind the honeymoon effect of the Tobin tax is as follows. If the fundamental x_t always remained in the interval $[-2n\tau, 2n\tau]$, then the government could keep the exchange rate at the central parity without any sacrifice in terms of interest rate.[9] In other words, if market participants were sure that the difference between the foreign interest rate and the desired domestic interest rate would never exceed $2n\tau$ %, the government would be able to insulate completely the exchange rate from external shocks. In this model, however, complete insulation cannot arise because

---

[8] The details are available on request.

[9] It is easy to check that $S_\tau(\cdot) = 0$ is the solution (28) in this case.

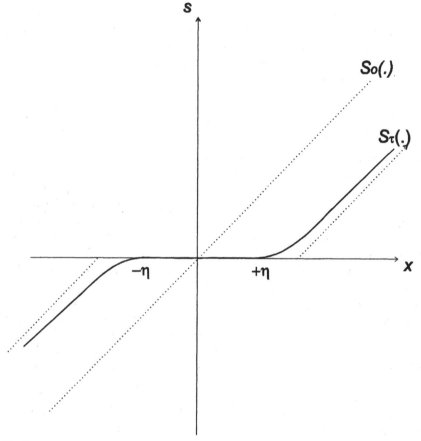

Fig. 1.

the fundamental x follows a stochastic process which may drive it outside of the range $[-2n\tau, 2n\tau]$. The expectation that the fundamental might go outside of this range puts some pressure on the exchange rate even when the fundamental is lower than $2n\tau$.

IV. Application to the EMS

The empirical part of this paper is based on a calibration of the model derived from the behaviour of the French franc between January 1991 and July 1993. During the sample period the franc was free of capital controls (they were removed in 1990), and its ERM central parity was not realigned. Thus, the French franc was in a situation close to that described in the model. Moreover, the franc was attacked repetitively (in September 1992, in the first quarter of 1993 and in July 1993) before it had to leave the narrow margins of the ERM in August 1993.[10] This makes it especially interesting to see what would have happened to the franc if it has been protected by a Tobin tax. We consider a very moderate tax rate, $\tau = 0.1\%$.

Data and Calibration

The model was calibrated using monthly data on the French and German one-month nominal interest rates and the log deviation of the FF/DM exchange rate from central parity. These data were constructed as the monthly averages of their daily counterparts, as they are collected each day at 11:30 a.m. by the Banque de France. The calibration given in Table 1 was derived as follows.

Equations (6) and (7) imply that the exchange rate relative to central parity follows the first-order autoregressive process:

$$s_t = \rho s_{t-1} + \varepsilon_{st} \tag{30}$$

so that an estimate of ρ can be obtained by regressing s_t on its lagged value, which gives $\hat{\rho} = 0.956$ (t-student = 16.46).

Using equations (2) and (4), the expected rate of realignment may be expressed as a function of the interest rate differential and the exchange rate relative to central parity:

$$E_t(c_{t+1} - c_t) = \frac{i_t - i_t^*}{n} - E_t(s_{t+1} - s_t) = \frac{i_t - i_t^*}{n} + (1-\rho)s_t. \tag{31}$$

The estimate of the expected rate of realignment given by this equation is exactly the same as that from the "drift adjustment method" developed by Bertola and Svensson (1993) and Svensson (1993). From (13), it follows that an estimate of α can be obtained by regressing the expected rate of realignment given by (31) on s_t, which gives $\hat{\alpha} = 0.107$ (t-student = 8.24).

Table 1.

ρ	α	q	σ
0.95	0.1	30	0.75

[10] Moutot (1994) provides a detailed account of the successive stages of the French franc crisis.

While the orders of magnitude of α and ρ are easy to obtain, the estimation of q and σ is more delicate because the desired domestic interest rate $\hat{\imath}$ is unobservable. Thus q and σ were not estimated but calibrated as plausibly as possible. Equation (7) implies $i_t^*-\hat{\imath}_t = [n^2(1-\alpha-\rho)+q]ns_t$. As Figure 2 shows, s_t was about 1% on average and fluctuated between 0 and 2% during the sample period. Taking $q = 30$ means that the differential between the foreign and the desired interest rates is assumed to have been about 2% on average, and not larger than 4% during the sample period. In several simulations, we have ensured that our results are not very sensitive to the value of q.

Equation (7) implies that the volatility of the shock in x is related to the volatility of the shock in s through:

$$\sigma = \frac{n^2(1-\alpha-\rho)+q}{n}\sigma_s. \tag{32}$$

Regression (30) provides the estimate $\hat{\sigma}_s = 0.389\%$. Whence given $\alpha = 0.1$, $\rho = 0.95$, $q = 30$ and $n = 12$, the estimate of σ is equal to 0.739%.

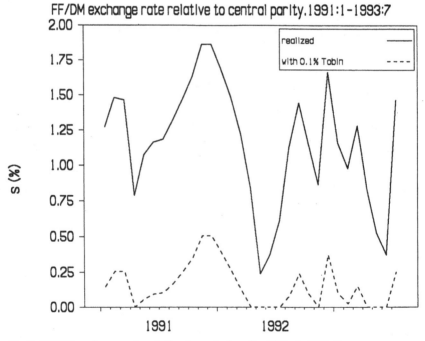

Fig. 2. FF/DM exchange rate relative to central parity, 1991:1–1993:7.

Results

The calibrated coefficients satisfy $\alpha + \rho > 1$, which implies that the French government had to increase the nominal interest rate when the desired level decreased. To illustrate, Figure 3 shows the French and German realized interest rates as well as the French desired interest rate during the sample period, as derived from equation (7).

A clear feature of the period is that the desired level of the interest rate was always lower in France than in Germany. According to most accounts, the policy misalignment resulted from German monetary unification, which induced a rise in i^*, and the low inflation associated with rising unemployment in France, which lowered the desired domestic interest rate $\hat{\imath}$. As a result, the French franc was always in the upper part of the band, and realignment expectations were chronic. The lack of credibility of the franc appears clearly in the FF/DM interest rate differential at the end of 1992 and during the first quarter of 1993.

How would a Tobin tax have benefited the French franc? Figures 2 and 3 allow us to compare the evolution of the exchange rate and the nominal interest rate in the presence of a 0.1% Tobin tax with the realized levels of

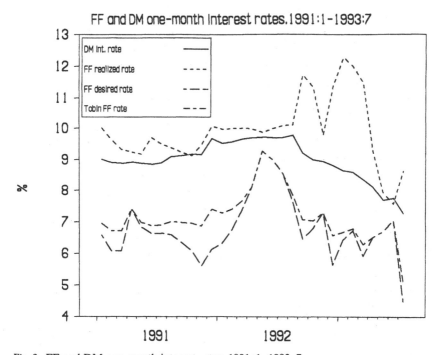

Fig. 3. FF and DM one-month interest rates, 1991:1–1993:7.

these variables.[11] It appears that the tax would have put the exchange rate relative to central parity close to 0.15%, i.e., less than a fifth of the realized level. The expected rate of realignment, which is proportional to the exchange rate relative to central parity, would also have been divided by a factor of five. Moreover, Figure 3 shows that the tax would have given the government considerable maneuverability in the implementation of monetary policy. The tax would have allowed the government to adjust the nominal interest rate in the desired direction, and keep it quite close to the desired level. As a result, the average value of the government's loss function would have been divided by more than thirty.

V. Concluding Comments

The message of this paper may be summarized in the following two points. First, at the theoretical level, a Tobin tax can stabilize a fixed exchange rate system by increasing the monetary independence enjoyed by the member countries. Second, at the empirical level, the stabilizing benefit of a small Tobin tax may be large.

It should be noted that these findings, even though they lend some support to the case of the Tobin tax, remain quite insufficient to support any specific policy recommendation. Even if the Tobin tax were feasible, which is far from having been established, it would remain to compare its benefits with its costs. This is a difficult task, if only because some costs of the Tobin tax, for example those pertaining to the international competition between financial centres, are delicate to assess. This would also require considering a number of different models in order to capture the different aspects of the problem. Our finding that the benefit of a Tobin tax is potentially large suggests that these questions are worth investigating.

Leaving aside the need for a more exhaustive cost-benefit analysis, there are several paths of research along which our analysis of the Tobin tax could be extended. First, it might be interesting to consider more general government objective functions than the one we have adopted here. For example, long-term interest rates may be introduced into the government's objective function. In the empirical part of this paper we have identified the interest rate which appears in the loss function with the one-month nominal interest rate. This assumption makes sense insofar as the mone-

---

[11] In order to construct Figures 2 and 3, we approximated numerically the solution to equation (28) using the following method. First, we discretized equation (29) with a discretization step of 0.01%, so that function $S_\tau(\cdot)$ could be described by a 500 dimensional vector in the interval [0%, 5%]. We then iterated (29) starting from the initial function $S_\tau^{(0)}(\cdot) = S_0(\cdot)$ until the sequence $S_\tau^{(k)}(\cdot)$ converged. Thirty iterations were sufficient to obtain convergence.

tary policy instrument is a short-term interest rate. However, one may argue that the government cares about interest rates because of their impact on the real economy, which comes essentially from the long-term interest rates. Including long-term interest rates in the analysis is likely to reduce the stabilizing effect of a Tobin tax, since this tax insulates short-term interest rates from external shocks to a larger extent than long-term interest rates.

While we have limited ourselves to a Tobin tax, the target zone model presented here can lend itself to the analysis of other types of capital controls. Such capital controls may be easier to implement than a Tobin tax,[12] and may have different stabilizing properties. In general, capital controls will be stabilizing in the context of our model to the extent that they allow the government to insulate its monetary policy from the foreign exchange constraint. An interesting path for further research would be to compare, in the context of our model, the stabilizing properties of the different types of capital controls which have been used or advocated.

Finally, our model exhibits some properties which are interesting in their own right, in particular the possibility of multiple equilibria. It would be interesting to interpret the conditions under which multiple equilibria arise, and to study empirically whether the behaviour of exchange rates in target zones supports the existence of sunspots. Another interesting topic would be to assess the extent to which a Tobin tax can remove multiplicity in this type of models. We plan to explore these questions in future research.

References

Bensaid, B. and Jeanne, O.: Fragilité des systèmes de change fixe et contrôle des capitaux. Forthcoming in *Economie et Prévision*, 1996.

Bertola, G. and Svensson, L. E. O.: Stochastic devaluation risk and the empirical fit of target-zone models. *Review of Economic Studies 60*, 689–712, 1993.

Dellas, H. and Stockman, A.: Self-fulfilling expectations, speculative attack, and capital controls. *Journal of Money, Credit and Banking 25*, 721–30, 1993.

Eichengreen, B. and Wyplosz, C.: The unstable EMS. *Brookings Papers on Economic Activity 1*, 51–143, 1993.

Eichengreen, B., Tobin, J. and Wyplosz, C.: Two cases for sand in the wheels of international finance. *Economic Journal 105*, 162–72, 1995.

Frankel, J.: How well do foreign exchange markets functions: Might a Tobin tax help? Paper presented at the conference on New and Innovative Sources of Financing Development, United Nations Development Programme, New York, Oct. 10, 1995.

---

[12] For example, Eichengreen, Tobin and Wyplosz (1995) propose a tax on lending to nonresidents, which may be easier to implement than the Tobin tax because it does not need to be universal. This tax can be levied in one country because it applies to resident lenders only.

Garber, P. and Taylor, M. P.: Sand in the wheels of foreign exchange markets: A sceptical note. *Economic Journal 105*, 173–80, 1995.

Jeanne, O.: Models of currency crises: A tentative synthesis, with special reference to the 1992–3 EMS crises. Mimeo, CERAS, Paris, 1995.

Kenen, P. B.: Capital controls, the EMS and EMU. *Economic Journal 105*, 181–92, 1995a.

Kenen, P. B.: The feasibility of taxing foreign-exchange transactions. Paper presented at the conference on New and Innovative Sources of Financing Development, United Nations Development Programme, New York, Oct. 10, 1995b.

Krugman, P.: Target zones and exchange rate dynamics. *Quarterly Journal of Economics 106*, 311–25, 1991.

Laskar, D.: "Time inconsistency" of the optimal monetary policy: A case for target zones. Mimeo, CEPREMAP, Paris, 1994.

Moutot, P.: Les caractéristiques et la gestion des tensions de change: le cas du Franc en 1992–3. *Cahiers Economiques et Monétaires 43*, 215–40, 1994.

Obstfeld, M.: Destabilizing effects of exchange rate escape clauses. NBER WP 3603, 1991.

Ozkan, G. and Sutherland, A.: Policy options for a currency crisis. *Economic Journal 105*, 510–19, 1995.

Park, D. and Sachs, J. D.: Capital controls and the timing of exchange regime collapse. NBER WP 2250, 1987.

Portes, R.: EMS and EMU after the fall. *World Economy 16*, 1–15, 1993.

Sargent, T. J.: *Dynamic Macroeconomic Theory.* Harvard University Press, Cambridge, MA, 1987.

Svensson, L. E. O.: Assessing target zone credibility: Mean reversion and devaluation expectations in the ERM, 1979–1992. *European Economic Review 37*, 763–802, 1993.

Svensson, L.: Why exchange rate bands? Monetary independence in spite of fixed exchange rates. *Journal of Monetary Economics 33*, 157–99, 1994a.

Svensson, L.: Fixed exchange rates as a means to price stability: What have we learned? *European Economic Review 38*, 447–68, 1994b.

Tobin, J.: A proposal for international monetary reform. *Eastern Economic Journal 4*, 153–9, 1978.

Wyplosz, C.: Capital controls and balance of payment crises. *Journal of International Money and Finance 5*, 167–79, 1986.

Financial Market Integration and Macroeconomic Volatility

Alan Sutherland*

University of York, Heslington, York YO1 5DD, England

Abstract

The process of financial market integration is modelled in an intertemporal general equilibrium framework as the elimination of trading frictions between financial markets in different countries. Goods markets are assumed to be imperfectly competitive and goods prices are subject to sluggish adjustment. Simulation experiments show that increasing financial market integration increases the volatility of a number of variables when shocks originate from the money market, but decreases the volatility of most variables when shocks originate from real demand or supply.

I. Introduction

The objective of this paper is to determine whether financial market integration leads to greater volatility of economic variables. There are a number of different ways to regard the process of financial market integration. One is to see it as a result of a reduction in frictions which prevent the free flow of finance across international borders. These frictions may take the form of government imposed rules or taxes on cross-border financial transactions. Financial integration may therefore arise directly from a policy decision to liberalise financial markets. This is clearly one factor behind the process of global financial market integration in the last few decades. It is also a major force leading to integration of financial markets within the European Union. But government policy is not the only factor at work in financial market integration. Changes in technology and institutional structure have also played an important role in increasing the ease with which agents in one country can operate in the financial markets of another.

The above-mentioned factors relate to frictions in financial markets. An alternative way of thinking about financial market integration is related to portfolio decisions by agents. Even when there are no trading frictions, it is possible that agents will choose largely to trade only in their own domes-

---

* This is a revised version of Sutherland (1996), I am grateful to the editors, two anonymous referees, and participants at seminars at York, Copenhagen and Manchester Universities for helpful comments and suggestions.

tic asset markets. This is because agents may find that domestic assets provide a better hedge against shocks than foreign assets. Clearly if two countries converge, so that they tend to face the same shocks, the hedging properties of their assets will converge and agents will hold more foreign assets in their portfolios. This process may be described as financial market integration.

It should be apparent that the first form of financial market integration (i.e., that which results from a reduction in trading frictions) is a factor which will have repercussions for the dynamic adjustment of the economy. The second type of financial market integration is a process which results from a change in the stochastic environment, i.e., it is a *symptom* rather than a *cause* of change. For these reasons this paper concentrates on the first form of financial market integration.

To the extent that financial market integration is a result of policy choices (as it is in Europe), it is of great importance to determine whether or not integration leads to greater volatility. Existing economic theory does not give a clear answer to this question. The Dornbusch (1976) model of exchange rate dynamics, for instance, appears to support a negative view of increased financial integration. Dornbusch's model suggests that freely operating foreign exchange markets will cause the nominal and real exchange rates to overshoot in response to a monetary shock. The real economy will consequently be destabilised by free capital mobility. On the other hand, it is often argued that *ad hoc* models, such as the Dornbusch model, do not fully take the role of financial markets into account. Financial markets give economic agents the opportunity to substitute consumption and leisure intertemporally and to share risks. Increased financial market integration may therefore allow agents to deal more effectively with random shocks. Models based on intertemporally optimising agents, such as those analysed by Frenkel and Razin (1987), would suggest that unambiguous benefits are to be gained by reducing barriers to the free movement of finance.

Typically, general equilibrium models incorporating intertemporal optimisation are constructed on the basis of perfectly functioning goods and labour markets. One of the crucial mechanisms at work in the Dornbusch model, however, is the interaction between sluggish adjustment of goods prices and rapid adjustment in financial markets. Intertemporal optimising models could therefore be giving a misleading picture of the effects of financial market integration because they fail to take account of imperfections elsewhere in the economic system.

This paper develops a model based on Obstfeld and Rogoff (1995) as a framework for considering this issue further. Obstfeld and Rogoff construct a two-country intertemporal general equilibrium model with imperfect competition in the goods market and nominal inertia generated by single period contracts. In this paper, two modifications to the model are made to allow more detailed study of financial market integration and nominal inertia. First, financial capital is made less than perfectly mobile across international boundaries. Second, multiperiod nominal contracts are introduced to allow consideration of varying degrees of nominal inertia.

As indicated above, this analysis models the process of financial market integration as arising from a reduction in trading frictions between financial markets in different countries. Here trading frictions take the form of costs of adjustment to asset stocks. To investigate the effects of varying the degree of market integration, the model is subjected to three forms of shocks: money supply, government purchases and labour supply. Volatility is measured by considering the impact effect of the three forms of shocks on macroeconomic variables.

The model is described in Section II. Section III presents the results and Section IV concludes the paper.

II. The Model

There are two equal sized countries each populated by consumers and producers. Consumers are identical, so the analysis can proceed by considering a representative individual from each country. Each firm produces a single differentiated product and is indexed by z on the unit interval. Goods are produced using labour supplied by consumers. There is no real capital.

Consumers and the Goods Market

The representative consumer in each country maximises a utility function which is defined over a CES basket of goods, C, real money balances, M/P, and labour supply, N. For the domestic consumer utility is given as:

$$U_t = \sum_{s=t}^{\infty} \beta^{s-t} \left[\frac{\sigma}{\sigma-1} C_s^{(\sigma-1)/\sigma} + \frac{\chi}{1-\varepsilon} \left(\frac{M_s}{P_s}\right)^{1-\varepsilon} - \frac{\kappa_s}{\mu} N_s^{\mu} \right] \tag{1}$$

where $0<\beta<1$, $\mu>1$ and σ, $\varepsilon>0$. Utility is defined identically for the foreign consumer. In what follows foreign variables are indicated by an asterisk. κ is a shock variable. An increase in κ represents an increase in the marginal disutility of labour and therefore a contraction in labour supply at a given wage.

The consumption index, C, is defined over all goods (both domestic and foreign produced) as:

$$C = \left[\int_0^1 c(z)^{(\theta-1)/\theta} \, dz \right]^{\theta/(\theta-1)} \tag{2}$$

where $\theta > 1$ and $c(z)$ is consumption of good z.

Purchasing power parity holds for each individual good so

$$p(z) = Ep^*(z) \tag{3}$$

where $p(z)$ is the domestic currency price of good z, E is the nominal exchange rate (defined as the domestic currency price of foreign currency) and $p^*(z)$ is the foreign currency price of good z.[1] It is assumed that goods indexed between 0 and 1/2 are domestically produced and goods indexed 1/2 and above are foreign produced. The general price index for domestic consumers, P, is therefore:

$$P = \left[\int_0^1 p(z)^{1-\theta} \, dz \right]^{1/(1-\theta)} = \left[\int_0^{1/2} p(z)^{1-\theta} \, dz + \int_{1/2}^1 Ep^*(z)^{1-\theta} \, dz \right]^{1/(1-\theta)} \tag{4}$$

PPP and identical preferences ensure that

$$P = EP^* \tag{5}$$

where P^* is the general price index for the foreign consumer.

Consumers and the Financial Market

A crucial assumption in this model is that the financial markets in the two countries are not perfectly integrated. The domestic consumer can therefore hold wealth in three forms: domestic bonds (which are only traded in the domestic financial market), domestic money and foreign bonds (which are only traded in the foreign financial market).[2] It is assumed that the domestic consumer can adjust holdings of domestic bonds without cost, whereas foreign asset holdings are subject to costs of adjustment. In a

---

[1] There is clearly a major asymmetry between the way goods and financial markets are treated in this model. The effects of the degree of integration of financial markets is considered against the background of perfect goods market integration. If goods markets are not perfectly integrated, purchasing power parity will not hold and firms might adopt a strategy of pricing to markets, as in Betts and Devereux (1996). The interaction between goods and financial market integration in a model of this form is likely to be an interesting topic for further work.

[2] It is assumed that the domestic consumer does not receive any liquidity benefits from holding foreign currency. Foreign currency is therefore dominated by foreign bonds. The same assumptions apply to the foreign consumer as regards holdings of domestic currency.

similar way, the foreign consumer has free access to the foreign bond market and is subject to adjustment costs in the domestic bond market.

There are many types of costs involved in transacting in foreign financial markets and each will have different implications for the form of the adjustment cost function. The most obvious form of adjustment costs are broker's fees. Typically, such fees are less than proportional to the size of transactions so some form of non-convexity in adjustment costs is suggested. However, many other types of costs arise in financial transactions. For instance, agents must devote resources to collecting information about investment opportunities and regulations in foreign markets. Communication systems have a fixed capacity in the short run, so attempts to transfer funds rapidly will cause congestion costs. Governments may impose regulations or taxes on foreign financial transactions. Technological costs, and to some extent learning costs and government regulations, may tend to make adjustment costs convex. On the other hand, some elements of the technology and learning processes are clearly one-off set-up costs.

The different forms of adjustment costs clearly imply different optimal dynamic behaviour for asset stocks. Convex adjustment costs will tend to encourage consumers to spread the adjustment of asset stocks over a period of time, with the optimal amount of adjustment related to the differential between the yields on domestic and foreign bonds.

Non-convexities in the adjustment cost function will tend to cause discontinuous adjustment of asset stocks. There will be a range of yield differentials where the incentive to adjust is too small to induce any movement of funds. But beyond certain trigger levels of the yield differential, adjustment will be rapid. The net result will be that the yield differential will not move much outside the range defined by the optimal trigger points. The more important the adjustment costs, the wider the band between the trigger points and the wider the range of fluctuation of yield differentials.[3]

For the purposes of this paper the differences between these forms of adjustment costs are not very important. When adjustment costs are large, the different forms of costs have approximately the same implication, i.e., the yield differential between domestic and foreign bonds will fluctuate over a relatively wide range and will not induce a strong a flow of funds between countries. For analytical convenience adjustment costs are

---

[3] If costs take the form of one-off lump-sum investment in infrastructure and knowledge, then adjsutment will again be discontinuous. But in this case one large shock will be sufficient to trigger investment in infrastructure and knowledge, so costs of this type will only be a temporary friction.

assumed to be convex.[4] More specifically, adjustment costs (in terms of the composite good) are given by

$$Z_t = \tfrac{1}{2}\psi I_t^2 \tag{6}$$

where I_t is the level of funds (in terms of the composite good) transferred from the domestic to the foreign bond market in period t. The process of financial market integration is represented by reducing the parameter ψ.

Holdings of domestic bonds are denoted by D (denominated in domestic currency) and holdings of foreign bonds are denoted by F (denominated in foreign currency). The domestic consumer's holdings of domestic bonds evolve according to

$$D_t = (1+i_{t-1})D_{t-1}+M_{t-1}-M_t+w_tN_t-P_tC_t-P_tI_t-P_tZ_t+\Pi_t-P_tT_t \tag{7}$$

where i is the nominal interest rate on domestic bonds, w is the nominal wage, Π is the consumer's share of profits of domestic firms and T is taxation. The evolution of foreign bond holdings is given by

$$F_t = (1+i^*_{t-1})F_{t-1}+P^*_tI_t \tag{8}$$

The first-order conditions relating to the consumer's maximisation problem are:

$$C_{t+1} = C_t\left[\beta(1+i_t)\frac{P_t}{P_{t+1}}\right]^\sigma \tag{9}$$

$$c_t(z) = \left[\frac{p_t(z)}{P_t}\right]^{-\theta} C_t \tag{10}$$

$$\frac{\chi(M_t/P_t)^{-\varepsilon}}{C_t^{-1/\sigma}} = \frac{i_t}{1+i_t} \tag{11}$$

$$\kappa_tN_t^{\mu-1} = C_t^{-1/\sigma}\frac{w_t}{P_t} \tag{12}$$

$$(1+i_t)(1+\psi I_t) = \frac{E_{t+1}}{E_t}(1+i^*_t)(1+\psi I_{t+1}) \tag{13}$$

An analogous set of conditions can be obtained for the foreign consumer. Equation (9) is the consumption Euler equation while (10) is the demand

---

[4] See Christiano and Eichenbaum (1992) for a previous example of a portfolio allocation problem modelled with convex costs of adjustment.

for individual product z. Equation (11) equates the marginal utility of real balances to the opportunity cost in terms of consumption.

Equation (12) is the labour supply rule which equates the marginal disutility of labour to the marginal utility of the real wage. There are assumed to be perfectly competitive, but separate, labour markets in each country. Nominal wages are determined by market clearing in the appropriate national labour market.

Equation (13) is the optimality condition relating to the allocation of wealth between domestic and foreign bonds. In effect (13) equates the rates of return on domestic and foreign bonds after adjusting for the costs of transferring funds between markets. Note that setting $\psi = 0$ reduces (13) to the standard uncovered interest parity condition.

The Government

The government in each country purchases goods in the form of the composite good and finances expenditure using lump-sum taxes and money printing. Thus

$$P_t G_t = P_t T_t + M_t - M_{t-1} \tag{14}$$

where G is purchases of the composite good.

Firms

Firm z faces a demand for its product given by:

$$y_t(z) = \left[\frac{p_t(z)}{P_t}\right]^{-\theta} Q_t \tag{15}$$

where $Q_t = [C_t + C_t^* + G_t + G_t^* + Z_t + Z_t^*]/2$. For simplicity it is assumed that output is equal to labour input. Thus

$$y_t(z) = N_t(z) \tag{16}$$

where $N(z)$ is labour input in the production of product z. Period t profits are therefore given by

$$\frac{\Pi_t(z)}{P_t} = \frac{p_t(z)}{P_t}\left[\frac{p_t(z)}{P_t}\right]^{-\theta} Q_t - \frac{w_t}{P_t}\left[\frac{p_t(z)}{P_t}\right]^{-\theta} Q_t \tag{17}$$

It is assumed that firms are subject to sluggish price adjustment of the form described by Calvo (1983a, b). According to this framework, in each period a fixed proportion of firms, γ, will leave their prices at the level inherited from the previous period, while the remaining $1 - \gamma$ reset their prices to a new optimal level. Thus for an individual firm there is probability γ that it will not adjust its price in the current period and a probability $1-\gamma$ that it will. The presence of this form of price inertia means that the price set in the current period may have an impact on profits in future periods. A firm which does adjust its price level in period t will maximise the discounted value of current and future profits with each future period weighted by the probability that the current price will still be in force in that period. Firm z's maximand is thus

$$V_t(z) = \sum_{s=t}^{\infty} \gamma^{s-t} R_{t,s} \frac{\Pi_s(z)}{P_s} \tag{18}$$

where $R_{t,s}$ is the discount factor between time t and time s. The first-order condition for firm z is

$$p_t(z)(\theta-1) \sum_{s=t}^{\infty} \gamma^{s-t} R_{t,s} \frac{Q_s}{P_s}\left(\frac{1}{P_s}\right)^{-\theta} = \theta \sum_{s=t}^{\infty} \gamma^{s-t} R_{t,s} \frac{Q_s}{P_s}\left(\frac{1}{P_s}\right)^{-\theta} w_s. \tag{19}$$

The structure of price setting implies that every firm which alters its price in period t chooses the same price level. The number of domestic firms which set their prices in period t is $(1-\gamma)$. So $(1-\gamma)$ firms set price p_t. Likewise the number of firms that last set their price in period $t-1$ is $(1-\gamma)\gamma$, so $(1-\gamma)\gamma$ firms have price level p_{t-1}. It is therefore possible to define an index of prices for domestically produced goods as:

$$q_t = \left[(1-\gamma) \sum_{s=0}^{\infty} \gamma^s p_{t-s}^{1-\theta} \right]^{1/(1-\theta)} \tag{20}$$

(here p_t is used to denote the price level of all domestic firms setting prices at time t). Moreover, it is possible to derive the following expression for the aggregate output of domestic firms (and thus aggregate labour demand):

$$y_t = \left[\frac{q_t}{P_t}\right]^{-\theta} Q_t = N_t \tag{21}$$

(here y and N are used to denote aggregate output and employment levels). Similar relationships hold for the foreign country.

Summary of Equilibrium Relationships

Equilibrium is defined as sequences of prices, wage rates, consumption levels, etc. which: clear the labour market in each country in each period where labour demand is given by (21) and labour supply is given by (12);

clear the money market in each country in each period where the money supply is determined exogenously by the government and money demand is given by (11); satisfy the optimality conditions for consumption evolution given by (9); satisfy the optimality conditions for the choice of price level in each price level in each period given by (19); satisfying the optimality conditions for the international transfer of funds given by (13); and satisfy the intertemporal budget constraints for each country.

III. Simulation Results

The model just described combines a number of important features which are relevant to the issue under discussion. Consumption expenditure is determined by agents who are maximising an intertemporal utility function. The ability of consumers collectively in one country to substitute consumption intertemporally depends on their ability to borrow and lend funds to consumers in the other country. The presence of frictions in international financial transactions will therefore have important implications for consumption decisions.

On the supply side of the model there is a contract structure for goods prices which implies that the goods market does not clear period by period. Shocks to the economy therefore create short-run disequilibria which generate incentives for intertemporal substitution of consumption and labour supply. Again frictions in financial markets which prevent intertemporal substitution from occurring will have important implications.

As it is not possible to obtain a closed-form solution to the model, a calibrated and log-linearised version of the system is simulated numerically. The model is subjected to permanent asymmetric shocks from three sources: the money supply, government purchases and labour supply.[5] In each case deterministic dynamic solution paths are presented for different degrees of financial market integration.[6] The effects of different degrees of price stickiness are also investigated.

---

[5] Simulation experiments with temporary shocks showed few qualitative differences when compared to permanent shocks. Only asymmetric shocks are considered because (at least in this model) symmetric shocks do not give rise to international financial flows, i.e., financial market integration has no effect on the model's response to symmetric shocks.

[6] The presence of shocks is somewhat contradictory in the context of a deterministic model. If shocks are possible, agents should have some view about the probability distribution of the shocks and should build this knowledge into the optimisation process. The first-order conditions relating to an explicitly stochastic optimisation problem would be slightly different from those described in Section II. However, once one accepts that linearisation is useful, the differences between the stochastic and deterministic problems largely disappear (due to the certainty equivalence property of linear models). Furthermore it proves very convenient to investigate the behaviour of the model in terms of deterministic solution paths. The deterministic solution paths show the linkages and relationships between variables following a shock in a way which is easy to interpret. Stochastic simulations largely obscure this information.

The calibrated parameter values used in the simulations are as follows: $\beta = 1/1.05$, $\varepsilon = 9.0$, $\mu = 1.4$, $\sigma = 0.75$, $\theta = 6.0$ and $\chi = 1.0$. Most of these values are taken from Hairault and Portier (1993).[7] The parameter ψ, which measures the degree of financial market integration, and the parameter γ, which measures the degree of price stickiness, are chosen to illustrate different cases in the simulations reported below. Perfect financial market integration is represented by $\psi = 0$, while imperfect market integration is illustrated with $\psi = 5$. γ is set at 0.5 as a benchmark value. This represents an average delay between price adjustments of two periods.

Money Supply Shocks

The dynamic response to a permanent shock to the money supply is illustrated in Figure 1. The money supply of the domestic country is increased by 1 percent and the money supply in the foreign country is reduced by 1 percent. The money supply changes enter the economy through lump-sum transfers. In each panel the plot marked with dots is the case of perfect capital mobility ($\psi = 0$) and the plot marked with crosses is the case of imperfect capital mobility ($\psi = 5$). Only variables for the domestic economy are illustrated. The response of the foreign economy is a mirror image of the domestic economy.

To understand the results, it is easiest to begin by considering the case of perfect capital mobility. With perfectly integrated financial markets there is effectively only one interest rate. A perfectly asymmetric shock implies that the quantity of funds domestic agents want to lend (or borrow) is always identical to the quantity of funds foreign agents want to borrow (or lend). As a result, asymmetric shocks do not change interest rates. This is confirmed in the last panel of Figure 1 which shows the dynamic response of the real interest rate. The behaviour of the nominal interest rate is not shown, but it is qualitatively the same as the behaviour of the real rate. It is easy to see from the consumption Euler equation (9) that the response of domestic consumption to the money supply shock must be a once-and-for-all step change to a new long-run level; see the first panel of Figure 1.

The effect of the monetary shock on the exchange rate can be determined by considering the money market equilibrium conditions in the two countries (equation (11) and its foreign counterpart). Combining these equations with the PPP relationship and log-linearising yields

---

[7] See Sutherland (1996) for a more detailed discussion of these parameter values.

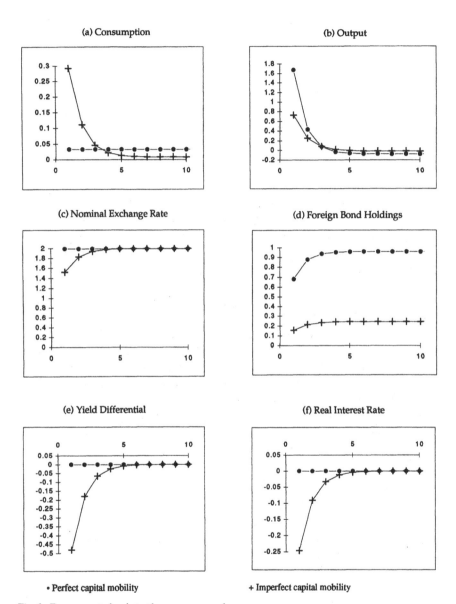

Fig. 1. Permanent shock to the money supply.
Note: Units of measurement:
    Consumption, output and the nominal exchange rate — Percentage deviation from
    initial equilibrium.
    Bond holdings — Deviation as percentage of initial consumption level.
    Interest rates — Percentage point deviation from initial equilibrium.

$$\hat{E}_t = \hat{M}_t - \hat{M}_t^* - \frac{1}{\sigma\varepsilon}[\hat{C}_t - \hat{C}_t^*] + \frac{\beta}{\varepsilon}[\hat{\iota}_t - \hat{\iota}_t^*] \tag{22}$$

where a hat indicates a log deviation from steady state. The shock to relative money supplies is a once-and-for-all step change. It has just been argued that relative consumption levels also make a once-and-for-all step change and that interest rates are unaffected by the shock. Equation (22) demonstrates that the exchange rate must also make a once-and-for-all step change in response to the monetary shock, as confirmed in Figure 1.

The fact that the nominal exchange rate depreciates while nominal prices are sticky implies that the relative price of domestically produced goods falls in the short run. The demand function for domestic goods (21) implies that this must result in a rise in domestic output. Again this is confirmed in Figure 1. As nominal contracts are renewed, relative prices and output move back towards their original levels. Domestic agents have high income in the short run while they maintain a flat consumption profile. They must therefore be saving and accumulating bonds, as shown in Figure 1, panel (d).[8]

Turn now to the case with imperfect capital mobility. The central implication of imperfect capital mobility is that domestic and foreign bonds become differentiated and can therefore pay different rates of return. The fact that domestic agents are attempting to accumulate assets drives down domestic interest rates (see the last two panels of Figure 1). Panel (e) shows the yield differential between domestic and foreign bonds, i.e., the nominal interest rate differential less the expected depreciation of the nominal exchange rate. The negative yield differential means that domestic and foreign consumers are induced to move funds into the foreign market.[9]

The fall in domestic real interest rates creates an incentive for domestic consumers to bring consumption forward in time. The first panel in Figure 1 shows that consumption rises sharply in period 1 and declines thereafter. Not surprisingly, in the absence of efficient ways of accumulating financial wealth, consumption follows the time profile of income very closely.

------

[8] All the effects just described are identical to those described by Obstfeld and Rogoff (1995). The full integration case in this model is identical to their model except for the extra dynamics introduced by multiperiod contracts.

[9] Figure 1 shows that the yield differential is only non-zero in the transitionary phase. In the long run, uncovered interest parity appears to be restored. It is important to point out, however, that these simulations only show deviations from steady state values. In an explicitly stochastic version of this model there can be a risk premium which implies a deviation from uncovered interest parity even in the steady state.

The behaviour of the exchange rate can again be explained with reference to (22). The consumption differential is much more strongly positive in the imperfect capital mobility case, while the interest differential becomes negative. Both effects imply that the exchange rate should not depreciate as much as in the perfect capital mobility case (also confirmed in Figure 1). The fact that the exchange rate depreciates by less in turn implies that the relative prices of domestic goods fall by less and domestic output rises by less.

What do these results imply for financial market integration and volatility? If volatility is measured by the impact effect of the shock then, in summary, increasing financial integration reduces the volatility of interest rates but increases the volatility of the nominal (and real) exchange rate. As a consequence, output is more volatile with integrated markets. Consumption, on the other hand, is less volatile because integrated financial markets provide more opportunities for consumption smoothing.

Goods Demand Shocks

The effect of a permanent asymmetric shock to government purchases is shown in Figure 2. In this case the domestic government increases expenditure by 1 percent and the foreign government reduces expenditure by 1 percent. The changes are financed by lump-sum taxes on consumers (i.e., domestic consumers pay more tax while foreign consumers pay less).

As in the previous case it is easiest to start by considering the results with perfect capital mobility. As before, when there is perfect capital mobility, an asymmetric demand shock has no impact on nominal and real interest rates. In turn this implies that the consumption response must be a once-and-for-all step change. Domestic consumers have a higher tax bill after the shock, so domestic consumption falls (by just over 0.34 percent; see the first panel of Figure 2).

Equation (22) can again be used to explain the behaviour of the nominal exchange rate. Relative money supplies and nominal interest rates have not changed following the shock, while the relative consumption level of domestic consumers has declined. The nominal exchange rate therefore depreciates. Panel (c) in Figure 2 shows a once-and-for-all depreciation of the exchange rate of 0.1 percent.

Since nominal prices are sticky in the short run, a nominal depreciation lowers the relative price of domestic goods. Domestic output therefore expands. Output also expands because the tax increase represents a negative wealth effect on domestic consumers. They therefore decrease their consumption of goods and leisure, i.e., labour supply expands. This is reflected in a higher long-run level of output. Output rises slightly less in the short run than in the long run. The flat consumption profile therefore

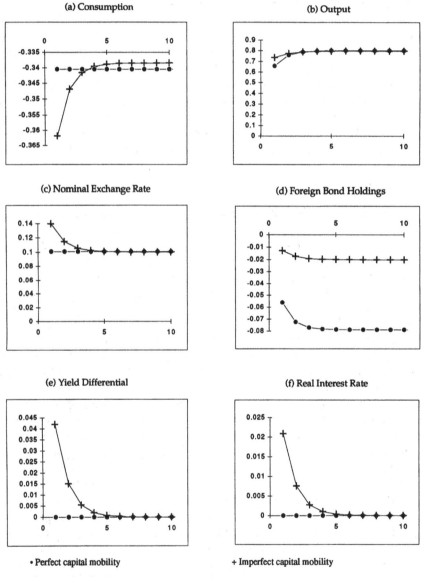

• Perfect capital mobility   + Imperfect capital mobility

Fig. 2. Permanent shock to government purchases.
Note: Units of measurement: see Figure 1.

implies some debt accumulation by domestic consumers in the short run; see panel (d) of Figure 2.

Consider now the implications of imperfect capital mobility. As just explained, the shock causes domestic consumers to accumulate debt. When financial markets are not perfectly integrated, debt accumulation must force up the interest rate in the domestic financial market. This is confirmed in the last two panels of Figure 2. High real interest rates in the short run, in turn, create an incentive for domestic consumers to shift consumption into the future, i.e., they adopt a rising consumption profile (see the first panel of Figure 2).

Equation (22) may also serve to analyse the response of the nominal exchange rate. Domestic interest rates have risen while relative consumption levels have fallen by more than in the perfect capital mobility case. The exchange rate must therefore depreciate by more in the short run, as shown in panel (c) of Figure 2. In turn a greater depreciation of the nominal exchange rate causes output to expand by more in the short run (panel (b) of Figure 2). Consumption and output now follow similar paths, so the consumer accumulates less debt (panel (d) of Figure 2).

In summary, the results in Figure 2 show that financial market integration stabilises all variables (except debt levels) in response to a demand shock in the sense that the short-run impact of the shock is smaller when there is perfect capital mobility.

Labour Supply Shocks

The effects of permanent shocks to labour supply are shown in Figure 3. In this case the parameter κ is increased by 1 percent for the domestic consumer and decreased by 1 percent for the foreign consumer. The domestic consumer therefore wants to supply less labour while the foreign consumer wants to supply more.

Consider first the case of perfet capital mobility. As in all previous cases, consumption makes a once-and-for-all step change in response to the shock. Not surprisingly, the reduction in labour supply leads to a long-run reduction in output. Therefore consumers also reduce consumption.

Equation (22) explains the effect on the nominal exchange rate. Interest rates and money supplies are unaffected by the shock while domestic consumption has declined relative to foreign consumption. The exchange rate therefore depreciates. As in previous cases with perfect capital mobility, the depreciation takes the form of a once-and-for-all step change.

The depreciation implies that the relative prices of home goods fall in the short run. This tends to offset the contraction in domestic output.

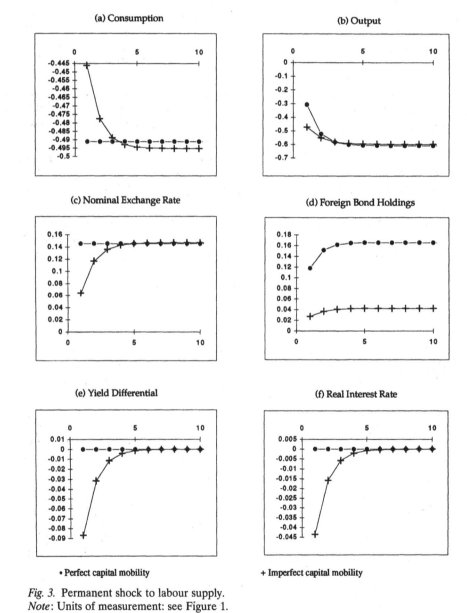

Fig. 3. Permanent shock to labour supply.
Note: Units of measurement: see Figure 1.

Output declines towards its new long-run level as nominal prices adjust to the shock. The fact that output is relatively higher in the short run while consumption falls allows domestic residents to accumulate assets.

Now consider the effects of imperfect capital mobility. The desire by domestic consumers to accumulate assets tends to drive down domestic interest rates and creates a yield differential in favour of foreign bonds. In turn this implies that consumers bring consumption forward in time. Consumption therefore falls by less in the short run compared to the perfect capital mobility case. Equation (22) shows that lower interest rates and higher consumption lead to a smaller depreciation of the nominal exchange rate in the short run; see panel (c) of Figure 3. Domestic goods prices therefore fall by less than in the perfect capital mobility case and output contracts by more in the short run.

In summary, the effect of moving to perfect capital mobility in the face of permanent labour supply shocks is to increase the short-run volatility of consumption and the nominal exchange rate, but to reduce the short-run volatility of output and nominal and real interest rates.

Varying the Degree of Price Inertia

A crucial feature of the Dornbusch (1976) model is the interaction between sluggish price adjustment in goods markets and high capital mobility. Sluggish price adjustment is also a crucial feature of the model under investigation here. The results just presented show that the behaviour of output is heavily dependent on the speed with which prices change. It was also seen that when there are frictions in financial markets, consumption is forced to follow the dynamic path of output more closely. The speed of price adjustment is therefore likely to have important implications for the effects of financial market integration.

Table 1 lists the impact effects of the different shocks for different values of the parameter γ. A lower value of γ implies that prices are more flexible. The benchmark value of $\gamma = 0.5$ yields an average delay between price adjustments of two periods. The effects of lowering γ to 0.25 imply an average delay of 1.33 periods between adjustments.

Table 1 also shows that the impact of monetary shocks on real variables declines as the degree of price inertia decreases — exactly as should be expected. In the absence of price inertia, the classical dichotomy holds in this model. On the other hand, demand and labour supply shocks have permanent real effects even when there are no price rigidities. In these cases price inertia tends to prevent real variables from adjusting quickly to their new long-run levels. The impact effects shown in Table 1 therefore increase when the degree of price inertia decreases.

Table 1. *Impact effects and price inertia*

γ	C		y		E		i		R	
Permanent money shocks										
0.25	0.00	0.13	0.60	0.25	2.00	1.77	0.00	−0.04	0.00	−0.15
0.50	0.03	0.32	1.67	0.62	1.99	1.47	0.00	−0.10	0.00	−0.27
Permanent demand shocks										
0.25	−0.34	−0.35	0.74	0.77	0.10	0.12	0.00	0.00	0.00	0.01
0.50	−0.34	−0.36	0.66	0.74	0.10	0.14	0.00	0.01	0.00	0.02
Permanent labour supply shocks										
0.25	−0.50	−0.47	−0.50	−0.55	0.15	0.11	0.00	−0.01	0.00	−0.02
0.50	−0.49	−0.44	−0.31	−0.49	0.14	0.06	0.00	−0.02	0.00	−0.05

Note: Each row corresponds to a value of γ. For each variable there are two columns, the first is for $\psi = 0$ and the second for $\psi = 5$.

The main feature of interest in Table 1 is the interaction between price inertia and capital mobility. In all cases, the differences between perfect and imperfect capital mobility increases as the degree of price inertia increases. This is most pronounced for monetary shocks.

The link between price inertia and capital mobility is straightforward to explain. The major implication of imperfect capital mobility is that it makes intertemporal substitution more difficult. This is more important when shocks have intertemporal effects on output. The main implication of price inertia is that it slows down the response of output to shocks. Therefore, the higher the degree of price inertia, the more agents want to use financial markets to smooth consumption. Hence the integration of financial markets will have a more significant impact when prices are sticky.

IV. Conclusion

The general picture that emerges from this study is that, with a few exceptions, increasing financial market integration tends to decrease short-run volatility. The main exception to this rule is the case of monetary shocks. Here financial integration tends to increase the short-run volatility of the nominal exchange rate and output. Yet even in this case financial integration reduces the volatility of nominal and real interest rates and consumption. Thus the analysis of this paper shows that some of the conclusions of the Dornbusch (1976) model do carry over to a more general model. But there are many important cases where they do not.

The model presented here can be improved in a number of directions. For instance, there are strong empirical and theoretical arguments for supposing that current account behaviour is driven in large part by capital accumulation; see Sachs (1981) and Baxter and Crucini (1993). The behaviour of capital stocks is therefore likely to have important implications for the effect of financial market integration. Another important modification to the model must be to relax the assumption of perfect goods market integration.

Another direction of improvement is in the measurement of welfare. This paper has, in effect, used volatility as a measure of welfare. But a truer measure of welfare is provided by the level of utility enjoyed by consumers. A utility based measure of welfare was not explicitly considered here since simulations of a linearised model are not well suited to such a task. Another important extension would therefore be a more rigorous analysis of welfare effects.

There is one final point which should be emphasised. This paper has considered the general equilibrium effects of increasing capital mobility. But this is not the only way to analyse the effects of market integration. It may be that market micro structure is much more important in determining the effects of greater integration. The day-to-day interaction between agents in financial markets may give rise to forces which far outweigh the effects identified in this paper.

References

Baxter, M. and Crucini, M.: Explaining savings-investment correlations. *American Economic Review 83*, 416–36, 1993.

Betts, C. and Devereux, M. B.: The exchange rate in a model of pricing-of-market. Forthcoming in *European Economic Review 40*, 1996.

Calvo, G.: Staggered prics in a utility-maximising framework. *Journal of Monetary Economics 12*, 383–98, 1983a.

Calvo, G.: Staggered contracts and exchange rate policy. In J. A. Frenkel (ed.), *Exchange Rates and International Macroeconomics*, University of Chicago Press, Chicago, 1983b.

Christiano, L. J. and Eichenbaum, M.: Liquidity effects and the monetary transmission mechanism. *American Economic Review (Papers and Proceedings) 82* 346–53, 1992.

Dornbusch, R.: Expectations and exchange rate dynamics. *Journal of Political Economy 84*, 1161–76, 1976.

Frenkel, J. A. and Razin, A.: *Fiscal Policies and the World Economy: An Intertemporal Approach*, MIT Press, Cambridge, MA, 1987.

Hairault, J.-O. and Portier, F.: Money, new-Keynesian macroeconomics and the business cycle. *European Economic Review 37*, 1533–68, 1993.

Obstfeld, M. and Rogoff, K.: Exchange rate dynamics redux. *Journal of Political Economy 103*, 624–60, 1995.

Sachs, J.: The current account and macroeconomic adjustment in the 1970's. *Brookings Papers on Economic Activity*, 201–68, 1981.

Sutherland, A.: Exchange rate dynamics and financial market integration. CEPR DP 1337, 1996.

Monetary Integration in Europe: Implications for Real Interest Rates and Stock Markets*

Matthew B. Canzoneri

Georgetown University, Washington, DC 20057-1045, USA

Harris Dellas

Catholic University of Leuven, B-3000 Leuven, Belgium

Abstract

We calibrate a simple general equilibrium model to assess the implications of financial market integration on real interest rates and equity prices in Germany, France, Italy and the U.K. We consider a flexible exchange rate regime, a hard EMS, and a common currency. We find that the effect of these regime changes on real interest rates (via the risk premium) should be small, but the effect on equity prices is potentially large. Moreover, the choice of central bank operating procedures may also be important for real interest rates.

I. Introduction

Monetary arrangements in Europe vacillated wildly over the last decade, and may be expected to continue to do so over the next.[1] What began as a loose confederation of currencies in the early 1980s hardened into a DM-zone in the late 1980s, and then loosened into what many characterize as a flexible rate system in the early 1990s.[2] The Maastricht Treaty calls for a common currency by the end of the decade; however, it is impossible to say whether this union will actually materialize.

Much of the literature on this chaotic process of regime switching has (quite rightly) focused on issues of credibility or macroeconomic stabilization. Here, we focus instead on the longer run implications of Europe's choice of monetary regime. Changing the way transactions are made —

---

* This paper was written while the first author was visiting the Bank of England. We gratefully acknowledge the Bank's financial support and intellectual stimulation, but the views expressed here are not necessarily shared by that institution.
[1] Alberto Giovannini describes this process as "regime making by fad".
[2] Indeed, the ERM's current 15% bands are wider than the 12% bands that McKinnon (1993) used to characterize the Plaza-Louvre agreement for the U.S. dollar.

that is, which currencies are used to buy what goods, and which currencies are linked to one another by official intervention — changes the way prices and exchange rates fluctuate in response to real and nominal shocks. Transaction patterns also determine the correlation between prices and consumption, which in turn affects real interest rates and the stock market via the risk premium. And finally, the changes in inflationary expectations that may accompany these regime switches can have an impact on the stock market via the seignorage tax. In this paper, we calibrate a simple general equilibrium model to assess the impact on Germany, France, Italy and the U.K. of the process of monetary integration — starting with a flexible rate regime, passing through a hard EMS, and ending in EMU, with periods of flexible rates along the way.

There is general agreement in Europe that a new central bank should inherit the Bundesbank's taste for low rates of inflation, but there is much less support for the Bundesbank's penchant for targeting monetary aggregates.[3] Most central banks are now using a nominal interest rate (in the short run) to target some combination of prices and output (in the longer run). The role of monetary aggregates has been downplayed because of the instability in velocity, except possibly in Germany, where for some reason velocity has been more stable.[4] We focus on the longer run, where prices and output respond to shocks and to monetary policy. Therefore, we generally assume that central banks are targeting nominal income; we view this as a reasonable compromise between price and output targets.[5] However, since so much weight is placed on the Bundesbank's view in discussions of EMU, we also ask what would happen if the new European central bank targeted a monetary aggregate instead.

In Section II, we specify a "world" economy consisting of the U.S. and "Europe". The latter consists of four countries: Germany, France, Italy and the U.K. In this model, goods produced in the various countries are assumed to be perfect substitutes, households are identical, and velocity is an exogenous stochastic process that has no effect on production or consumption.

This simple framework has its advantages and its disadvantages. The

---

[3] Indeed, one of the major tasks of the European Monetary Institute, which was created by the Maastricht Treaty as the precursor of a European central bank, is to study operating procedures.

[4] A discussion of the change in central bank operating procedures can be found in "Monetary Policy in the Wake of Financial Liberalization", which is an annex to the OECD document "Current Monetary Policy Issues", 1989. Goodfriend and Small (1993) provide detailed discussions of the operating procedures of a number of central banks.

[5] Nominal income targeting has its own advocates; see, for example, McCallum (1988).

advantages are clarity and ease of analysis. There is only one good in terms of which to define real interest rates. This has the advantage of isolating the effects of risk premia: the only thing that keeps real interest rates from equalizing across countries is the fact that bonds denominated in different currencies will have different *ex-post* rates of return, depending on how that currency's price level fluctuates in response to shocks. The disadvantages are obvious. The model lacks much of the richness of the real world. Households in different countries buy different consumption bundles, and they make savings decisions based on real interest rates defined in terms of those consumption bundles. Velocity is probably not an exogenous process; and its behavior may change in response to a regime switch. In addition, velocity shocks probably affect production and consumption. In Section IV, we discuss extensions to include domestic (non-traded) goods, slow price adjustment, and liquidity effects. However, in this paper we stick to the simple model because it has very clear implications for real interest rates and national stock markets.

In Section III, we use data on productivity and velocity to calibrate our model. In this way, we can see which of the insights gained in Section II are likely to be quantitatively important. Generally, we find that Europe's choice of monetary regime has a much smaller impact on risk premia than does the central bank's choice of targeting procedure. However, we also find that the changes in anticipated inflation that may accompany a regime switch can have a major impact on national stock markets, and we show that "news" about regime switches can be quite destabilizing.[6]

II. The Model

We begin with a three-country model consisting of the U.S., Germany and France; the extension to include Italy and the U.K. will be obvious. Consider a world populated by identical, infinitely lived households whose utility in period t is given by

$$U_t = E_t \sum_{j=t}^{\infty} \beta^{j-t} u(c_j), \tag{1}$$

---

[6] Moreover, regime switches can have a big impact on price stability and exchange rate stability, and not always in the directions that one might expect. In particular, the effect on price stability may be the opposite of the effect on exchange rate stability, since the latter depends on the covariance between U.S. and European price levels in addition to their individual volatilities. Price and exchange rate stability are discussed in Canzoneri and Dellas (1995b).

where $c_j = c_{gj} + c_{fj} + c_{aj}$ is consumption, $E(\cdot)$ is the expectation operator, and $u(\cdot)$ is a strictly concave function. German goods, c_{gj}, French goods, c_{fj}, and American goods, c_{aj}, are perfect substitutes for one another.

Each period is subdivided into a financial exchange and a goods exchange. In the financial exchange, households receive income and trade assets. In the goods exchange that follows, households trade money for goods; barter is not allowed and only the producer's currency is accepted. In the standard cash-in-advance model, a household can only spend the money that it holds at the end of the financial exchange. Income earned on the sale of goods in the current period is not available until the next financial exchange. This means that money turns over once, and velocity is fixed at unity. Here, we follow Woodford (1991) in assuming that the household can also spend a fraction α_h ($h = g, f$, or a) of its current income in country h; the rest becomes available in the next financial exchange. With this generalization, velocity can be greater than one. The fraction α_h measures the efficiency of a country's payments system. Woodford assumed that α_h is a fixed, exogenous parameter. We assume that α_h is exogenous, but we let it fluctuate randomly from period to period. This makes velocity exogenous and stochastic in each country.

The household's cash-in-advance constraints for period j are

$$m_{hj} + \alpha_{hj} p_{hj} s_{hj} X_{hj} \geq p_{hj} c_{hj}, \tag{2}$$

where $h = g, f, a$. Income comes in the form of dividends. Firms in country h produce (at zero cost) and sell output X_{hj}; they return the proceeds to their shareholders. X_{hj} is an exogenous random variable; we refer to it as the "productivity" shock or the "real" shock. s_{hj} is the household's share in the firms of country h, and $\alpha_{hj} p_{hj} s_{hj} X_{hj}$ is the fraction of the period j dividends that can be spent in period j.

The household's budget constraint in the financial exchange is

$$\sum_{h=g,f,a} \left[\left(\frac{m_{hj-1}}{p_{hj}} \right) + \left(\frac{\alpha_{hj-1} p_{hj-1} s_{hj-1} X_{hj-1}}{p_{hj}} \right) - \left(\frac{p_{hj-1} c_{hj-1}}{p_{hj}} \right) \right]$$

$$+ \sum_{h=g,f,a} \left(\frac{I_{hj-1} b_{hj-1}}{p_{hj}} \right) + \sum_{h=g,f,a} s_{hj-1} \left[(1 - \alpha_{ht-1}) \left(\frac{p_{hj-1} X_{hj-1}}{p_{hj}} \right) + q_{hj} \right]$$

$$+ \sum_{h=g,f,a} s_{hj-1} \left[\left(\frac{M_{hj} - M_{hj-1}}{p_{hj}} + Q_{hj} \right) \right]$$

$$\geq \sum_{h=g,f,a} \left[\left(\frac{m_{hj}}{p_{hj}} \right) + \left(\frac{b_{hj}}{p_{hj}} \right) + q_{hj} s_{hj} + Q_{hk} S_{hj} \right]. \tag{3}$$

m_{hj}, b_{hj}, s_{hj}, and S_{hj} are the household's demand for money, bonds, equity shares and money transfer shares. The latter entitle the owner to the money injections, $M_{hj} - M_{hj-1}$, that governments make each period; the transfers could be negative.[7] I_{hj} is the gross nominal interest rate on bonds; q_{hj} and Q_{hj} are the prices of equity shares and transfer shares. Equation (3) says that the money carried into the asset exchange, plus the gross return on bonds, equity shares and transfer shares must be able to pay for the purchase of new assets.

The household chooses c_{hj}, b_{hj}, m_{hj}, s_{hj}, and S_{hj} ($h = g, f, a$) to maximize (1) subject to (2) and (3). If (as we assume) nominal interest rates are positive, then the cash-in-advance constraints are binding, and the first-order conditions for period t become:

$$u'(c_t) = \lambda_t, \tag{4a}$$

$$1/I_{ht} = \beta E_t[(\lambda_{t+1}/\lambda_t)(p_{ht}/p_{ht+1})], \tag{4b}$$

$$q_{ht} = \alpha_{ht} X_{ht} + \beta E_t\{(\lambda_{t+1}/\lambda_t)[q_{ht+1} + (1 - \alpha_{ht})(p_{ht} X_{ht}/p_{ht+1})]\}, \tag{4c}$$

$$Q_{ht} = \beta E_t\{(\lambda_{t+1}/\lambda_t)[Q_{ht+1} + (M_{ht+1} - M_{ht})/p_{ht+1}]\}, \tag{4d}$$

where $h = g, f, a$, and λ_t is the Lagrange multiplier for the period t budget constraint. These are familiar asset pricing equations when α_{ht} is equal to zero; when α_{ht} is positive, part of the return on equity is available in the current period, and does not get discounted.

In the "pooled" equilibrium,

$$p_{at} = e_{gt} p_{gt} = e_{ft} p_{ft}, \tag{5a}$$

$$c_t = c_{gt} + c_{ft} + c_{at} = X_{gt} + X_{ft} + X_{at}, \tag{5b}$$

$$s_{ht} = S_{ht} = 1, \tag{5c}$$

$$M_{ht} = m_{ht} = p_{ht} X_{ht}/V_{ht}, \tag{5d}$$

where $h = g, f, a$, and $V_{ht} = (1 - \alpha_{ht})^{-1}$ is the "velocity" shock. Equation (5a) is the law of one price; e_{gt} and e_{ft} are dollar exchange rates. Each household has the same consumption pattern and the same asset portfolio.

The (*ex-ante*) real return on bonds is defined by

$$R_{ht} = I_{ht} E_t(p_{ht}/p_{ht+1}). \tag{6}$$

Equations (6) and (4c) can be rewritten to expose the risk premium.[8]

---

[7] We need such an asset to assure that a "pooled" equilibrium exists. We also assume that governments just issue money and bonds; we do not worry about the differential effects of taxes or spending.

[8] Here and elsewhere in the paper, we make use of the fact that $E(XY) = E(X)E(Y) + \text{Cov}(X, Y)$ for any two random variables, X and Y.

$$1/R_{ht} = \beta E_t[(u'(c_{t+1})/u'(c_t))(p_{ht}/p_{ht+1})]/E_t(p_{ht}/p_{ht+1}) \qquad (7a)$$

$$= 1/\bar{R}_t + \beta \, \text{Cov}_t[u'(c_{t+1})/u'(c_t), p_{ht}/p_{ht+1}]/E_t(p_{ht}/p_{ht+1}),$$

$$q_{ht} = \alpha_{ht}X_{ht} + \beta E_t\{[u'(c_{t+1})/u'(c_t)][q_{ht+1} + (1-\alpha_{ht})(p_{ht}X_{ht}/p_{ht+1})]\} \qquad (7b)$$

$$= \beta E_t\{[u'(c_{t+1})/u'(c_t)]q_{ht+1}\} + [1-(1/V_{ht})]X_{ht}$$

$$+ (1/V_{ht})[X_{ht}E_t(p_{ht}/p_{ht+1})]/R_{ht},$$

where

$$1/\bar{R}_{ht} = \beta E_t[u'(c_{t+1})/u'c_t)]. \qquad (8)$$

$\bar{R}_{ht}$ would be the real return on a risk free (or indexed) bond, if one existed. The covariance term in (7a) is the risk premium; it passes to (7b) via R_{ht}.

The risk premium depends on the correlation between prices and consumption. The *ex-post* return on a nominal asset varies inversely with the price level. If prices move countercyclically, then bonds pay well when consumption is high and poorly when consumption is low. Nominal assets are therefore lotteries that transfer income out of the high marginal utility states and into the low marginal utility states, decreasing expected utility. Lenders demand a premium over the return they would require on a risk free asset; this is the covariance term in (7a). If, on the other hand, prices move procyclically, the nominal assets transfer income the other way, and lenders grant a negative premium.

A portion, $1-\alpha_{ht}$, of the dividends representing the sale of current production is not available until the next financial exchange, when its real value will have been inflated away; these dividends bear the same risk as the nominal interest on bonds. These dividends are also affected by anticipated inflation, since the seignorage tax falls entirely on dividends in our model. These facts can be seen in (7b), where a portion of current production, $(1-\alpha_{ht})X_{ht}$, is discounted by both expected inflation (to obtain the after-tax return) and the real interest rate (to obtain the present value). Anticipated inflation lowers the expected return, and countercyclical price movements induce a risk premium for the reasons given above. Both factors are reflected in lower equity prices.

Consumption is determined by (5b) and price levels are determined by (5d). Productivity shocks drive both, and produce a negative correlation; so, risk premia are positive in our model.[9] Productivity shocks and velocity shocks drive prices and exchange rates. The size of risk premia and the

---

volatility of prices and exchange rates depend on the stochastic processes driving the shocks and the monetary regimes in place.

In what follows, we assume that utility takes the form

$$u(c) = \begin{cases} (c^{1-k}-1)/(1-k) & \text{for } 0 \leq k \neq 1 \\ \log(c) & \text{for } k = 1 \end{cases} \tag{9}$$

where k is the coefficient of relative risk aversion, and we assume that the stochastic processes for the shocks are given by

$$X_{hj} = X_{hj-1}x_{hj}, \tag{10a}$$

$$V_{hj} = V_{hj-1}v_{hj}, \tag{10b}$$

where the x_{hj}'s are independent of the v_{hj}'s and $E_t(x_{hj}) = E_t(v_{hj}) = 1$ for all $j > t$. This specification of the stochastic processes allows convenient aggregations and disaggregations. For example, we can define world output by

$$X_{wt} = X_{at} + X_{gt} + X_{ft} = X_{wt-1}x_{wt}, \tag{11}$$

where $x_{wt} = w_{at-1}x_{at} + w_{gt-1}x_{gt} + w_{ft-1}x_{ft}$ and $w_{ht-1} = X_{ht-1}/X_{wt-1}$. We define European output and velocity in an analogous manner.

Floating Exchange Rates

Central banks target nominal income. This means that velocity shocks are automatically accommodated, and $M_{ht}V_{ht}$ is guided along a target path. Let

$$M_{hj+1}V_{hj+1}/M_{hj}V_{hj} = \Pi_h, \tag{12}$$

where Π_h is the target rate of nominal income growth in country h. From (5b) and (5d), the growth in price levels and consumption is given by

$$p_{ht+1}/p_{ht} = \Pi_h/x_{ht+1}, \tag{13a}$$

$$c_{ht+1}/c_{ht} = x_{wt+1}. \tag{13b}$$

Π_h is also the anticipated rate of inflation.

Real interest rates and equity prices are given by

$$R_{ht,F} = E_t(x_{ht+1})/\beta E_t(x_{ht+1}x_{wt+1}^{-k}) = 1/\beta E_t(x_{ht+1}x_{wt+1}^{-k}), \tag{14a}$$

$$q_{ht,F} = \alpha_{ht}X_{ht} + \beta E_t\{x_{wj+1}^{-k}[q_{ht+1,F} + (1-\alpha_{ht})X_{ht}x_{ht+1}/\Pi_h]\} \tag{14b}$$

$$= \beta E_t(x_{wj+1}^{-k}q_{ht+1,F}) + [1-(1/V_{ht})]X_{ht} + (X_{ht}/V_{ht}\Pi_h R_{ht,F}).$$

The determinants of $R_{ht,F}$ can be seen more clearly by decomposing (14a) along the lines of equation (7):

$$1/R_{ht,F} = \beta E_t(x_{ht+1}x_{wt+1}^{-k}) \tag{15}$$

$$= \beta E_t(x_{ht+1}) E_t(x_{wt+1}^{-k}) + \beta \, \text{Cov}_t(x_{ht+1}, x_{wt+1}^{-k})$$

$$\approx \beta E_t[1 - k(x_{wt+1}-1) + \tfrac{1}{2}k(k+1)(x_{wt+1}-1)^2]$$

$$+ \beta \, \text{Cov}_t\{x_{ht+1}, 1 - k(x_{wt+1}-1)\}$$

$$= \beta[1 + \tfrac{1}{2}k(k+1)\text{Var}_t(x_{wt+1})] - \beta k \, \text{Cov}_t(x_{ht+1}, x_{wt+1}),$$

where x_{wt+1}^{-k} has been approximated around $x_w = 1$ ($= E_t(x_w)$). The covariance term in (15) approximates the risk premium; the first term approximates the risk free rate, $1/\bar{R}_{ht}$.

Two things matter for the level of real interest rates: the covariance between domestic output and world output, and the degree of relative risk aversion, k. Prices are driven (inversely) by domestic output, while consumption is driven (directly) by world output. So, prices will be negatively correlated with consumption, and nominal assets will pay a positive risk premium, if domestic output is positively correlated with world output. The more procyclical is domestic output, the bigger is the risk premium. Increasing risk aversion does two things: it increases the risk premium, which tends to raise $R_{ht,F}$, but it also lowers the risk free rate, $\bar{R}$, which tends to lower $R_{ht,F}$. The second effect dominates in the model calibrations of Section III.

Three things matter for equity prices: the correlation between domestic output and world output, the degree of relative risk aversion, and the trend rate of inflation. The first two have to do with the risk premium, and affect equity prices for the same reasons that they affect the real interest rate. The third is the seignorage tax, which falls on dividends and lowers equity prices. All of these factors are apparent in the last term of (14b).

A Hard EMS

Suppose now that France credibly fixes its exchange rate with Germany; the U.S. and Germany continue to target nominal income. If the exchange rate is pegged at unity, then the law of one price implies $p_{ft} = p_{gt}$. Equation (13a) still gives the inflation rates for the U.S. and Germany, and (13b) gives consumption growth for all three countries. Nothing has changed in the U.S. or Germany; only France is affected. In adopting German prices, France has also adopted German interest rates and German exchange rate volatility. French equity prices become

$$q_{ft,\text{EMS}} = \beta E_t(x_{wj+1}^{-k} q_{ft+1,\text{EMS}}) + [1 - (1/V_{ft})]X_{ft} + (X_{ft}/V_{ft}\Pi_g R_{gt,\text{EMS}}). \tag{16}$$

French assets now bear the German risk premium, and French dividends are taxed at the German inflation rate.

If $\Pi_f > \Pi_g$, then joining the EMS lowers trend inflation in France. This, of course, was the rationale for the "franc fort" policy, which seems to have survived the loosening of the ERM. One of the less heralded effects of lowering anticipated inflation should have been a rise in the value of the French stock market, due simply to the fall in seignorage taxes.

But, trend inflation is not the only issue here. The EMS forces France to do more than just lower trend money growth. The cash-in-advance constraints imply that

$$M_{ft}/M_{ft-1} = (M_{gt}/M_{gt-1})(v_{gt}/v_{ft})(x_{ft}/x_{gt}). \tag{17}$$

This is the growth in the French money supply that keeps the exchange rate fixed; the French must accommodate their own velocity and productivity shocks, and they must absorb the German shocks into their money supply and price level. This has implications for the French risk premium. If German output is more highly correlated with world output than is French output (and we will see that this is indeed the case), then the French risk premium should rise, causing the real interest rate to rise and the stock market to fall.

Summarizing, the implications of the "franc fort" policy are as follows. The French real interest rate rises (if German output is more highly correlated with world output than is French output), but the effect on the French stock market is ambiguous. Higher risk premia tend to lower its value, while the fall in anticipated inflation works in the other direction.

EMU

Suppose now that Europe adopts a common currency, denoted by M_{et}. Aggregating the French and German cash-in-advance constraints, we have in equilibrium

$$M_{et} = m_{et} = p_{et}X_{et}/V_{et}, \tag{18}$$

where

$$X_{et} = X_{gt} + X_{ft} = X_{et-1}x_{et} \tag{19a}$$

$$x_{et} = (X_{gt-1}/X_{et-1})x_{gt} + (X_{ft-1}/X_{et-1})x_{ft}, \tag{19b}$$

$$V_{et} = V_{gt} + V_{ft} = V_{et-1}v_{et}, \tag{19c}$$

$$v_{et} = (V_{gt-1}/V_{et-1})v_{gt} + (V_{ft-1}/V_{et-1})v_{ft}. \tag{19d}$$

Here, we are assuming that the processes for velocity and productivity are not affected by the formation of a monetary union. This assumption may be questionable in the longer run, especially in the case of velocity.

Suppose that the European central bank targets nominal income. The growth in prices and consumption becomes

$$p_{ht+1}/p_{ht} = \Pi_h/x_{ht+1}, \tag{20a}$$

$$c_{ht+1}/c_{ht} = x_{wt+1}, \tag{20b}$$

where $h = e, a$. These equations are analogous to (13a) and (13b). In Europe, real interest rates and equity prices are given by

$$R_{et, \text{EMU}} = 1/\beta E_t(x_{et+1} x_{wt+1}^{-k}), \tag{21a}$$

$$q_{ht, \text{EMU}} = \beta E_t(x_{wj+1}^{-k} q_{ht+1, \text{EMU}})$$

$$+ [1 - (1/V_{et})]X_{ht} + (X_{ht}/V_{et}\Pi_e R_{et, \text{EMU}}), \tag{21b}$$

where $h = g, f$. Now the European price level is driven by European output, and not just German output. If European output is less highly correlated with world output than is German output (as is indeed the case), then the European risk premium falls; the European real interest rate falls, and the value of the European stock market rises (assuming there has been no increase in the trend rate of inflation).

Suppose the European central bank targets money instead of nominal income. The only difference is that the European velocity shock will not be automatically accommodated. This does not affect the risk premium, since consumption is independent of velocity in this model.

III. Model Calibrations

The qualitative implications of our model are clear: (i) The risk premium on nominal assets depends on the correlation between the output driving the price level and the output driving consumption; if the correlation increases as we pass from one regime to another, then the (negative) correlation between the price level and consumption increases, raising the risk premium. The real interest rate rises and the stock market falls. (ii) Anticipated inflation lowers the value of equity in firms whose sales are denominated in that currency. A change in monetary regime that lowers anticipated inflation will raise the value of the stock market. In this section, we calibrate a "world" model — consisting of the U.S., Germany, France, Italy, and the U.K. — to assess the importance of the choice of an international monetary regime.

Suppose the innovations, x_{ht} and v_{ht}, in the processes for productivity and velocity are log normally distributed. We can calculate the real interest rates, equity prices, and measures of volatility given in the preceding section once the standard deviations of the innovations have been estimated and the values of k, β, V_h and Π_h have been specified.[10] We can set the discount factor at 0.96, and we can take historical averages for V_h and Π_h, but the coefficient of relative risk aversion, k, is much more difficult to specify.[11] We assume that the reasonable range for k is somewhere between one and four.

We can estimate the standard deviations of the innovations from the regressions given in Table 1. The periodicity of the model is not obvious on theoretical grounds. In the end, we chose to use annual data to avoid the "smoothing" inherent in seasonalized data. Reuven Glick and Kenneth Rogoff provided us with their data on productivity, these data are described fully in Glick and Rogoff (1993). The M1 velocity data were constructed from the IFS tapes. The regressions indicate that a random walk provides a reasonably good description of productivity and velocity data in all of the countries except Germany; as is often asserted, German velocity is more stable than the rest.

The variance-covariance matrix for the productivity innovations is given in Table 2; European and world aggregates were constructed using the weights given at the bottom of Table 2. These variances and covariances determine most of the results for risk premia and for the volatility of prices and exchange rates. It is worth noting at the outset how Germany compares with the other European countries. German output is less volatile than Italian output or British output, but more volatile than French output or European output as a whole. German output is less highly correlated with world output than is Italian output or British output, but more highly correlated than is French output. Its correlation with world output is virtually identical with that of European as a whole. Finally, German output is less highly correlated with U.S. output than is British output, about equally correlated as is Italian output, and more highly correlated than is French output.

Real interest rates are given in Table 3 for values of the coefficient of relative risk aversion ranging from 1 to 4. Columns 2 through 5 give the results for the flexible rates regime. Column 6 gives the results for the EMS; France, Italy and the U.K. fix their DM exchange rates while

[10] Real interest rates can be calculated directly by numerically integrating in the corresponding equations. The solutions for the stock prices are not amenable to explicit numerical integration due to the random walk assumption: the output shares that appear in these equations are non-linear functions of random walk variables. The procedure we use to calculate stock prices is as follows. We generate random numbers from a multivariate lognormal distribution with the variance-covariance structure described in Table 2. We take as initial values for outputs the corresponding shares, also reported in Table 2, and we simulate output paths for 100 years. We then use the simulated output paths in the stock price equations. The process is repeated 100 times, and the numbers reported are the averages from those 100 runs.

[11] See, for example, Hansen and Singleton (1983) and Mankiew and Zeldes (1991).

Table 1. *Stochastic processes for productivity and velocity*

Productivity	Velocity
U.S.	
$\ln(x_{t+1}) = 0.11 + 0.98 \ln(x_t)$ (0.10) (0.02)	$\ln(v_{t+1}) = 0.088 + 0.96 \ln(v_t)$ (0.043) (0.027)
$SEE = 0.029$ $R^2 = 0.99$ $DW = 1.5$	$SEE = 0.036$ $R^2 = 0.98$ $DW = 1.97$
Germany	
$\ln(x_{t+1}) = 0.23 + 0.95 \ln(x_t)$ (0.06) (0.01)	$\ln(v_{t+1}) = 1.03 + 0.43 \ln(v_t)$ (0.31) (0.17)
$SEE = 0.023$ $R^2 = 0.99$ $DW = 1.9$	$SEE = 0.043$ $R^2 = 0.13$ $DW = 1.78$
France	
$\ln(x_{t+1}) = 0.22 + 0.96 \ln(x_t)$ (0.02) (0.01)	$\ln(v_{t+1}) = -0.06 + 0.94 \ln(v_t)$ (0.08) (0.07)
$SEE = 0.018$ $R^2 = 0.99$ $DW = 1.79$	$SEE = 0.052$ $R^2 = 0.81$ $DW = 1.86$
U.K.	
$\ln(x_{t+1}) = 0.05 + 0.99 \ln(x_t)$ (0.09) (0.02)	$\ln(v_{t+1}) = -0.05 + 0.91 \ln(v_t)$ (0.03) (0.03)
$SEE = 0.028$ $R^2 = 0.99$ $DW = 1.34$	$SEE = 0.06$ $R^2 = 0.95$ $DW = 1.31$
Italy	
$\ln(x_{t+1}) = 0.18 + 0.97 \ln(x_t)$ (0.05) (0.01)	$\ln(v_{t+1}) = 0.06 + 0.93 \ln(v_t)$ (0.04) (0.04)
$SEE = 0.035$ $R^2 = 0.99$ $DW = 2.46$	$SEE = 0.064$ $R^2 = 0.92$ $DW = 1.34$

Notes: Productivity data are based on manufacturing industries and were provided by Glick and Rogoff; annual, 1960–90. Velocity data are based on M1 aggregates and were constructed from the IFS tapes; annual, 1950–90.

Table 2. *Variance covariance matrix of the productivity innovations*

	U.S.	Germany	France	U.K.	Italy	Europe	World
U.S.	0.00080	0.00026	0.00011	0.00051	0.00023	—	0.00058
Germany		0.00051	0.00022	0.00026	0.00030	0.00034	0.00029
France			0.00030	0.00023	0.00018	0.00023	0.00017
U.K.				0.00071	0.00019	0.00033	0.00044
Italy					0.00113	0.00041	0.00031
Europe						0.00015	0.00029
World							0.00029

Note: Output shares: U.S. = 0.57, Germany = 0.13, France = 0.11, U.K. = 0.10, Italy = 0.09.

Table 3. *Real interest rates*

k	Germany	France	U.K.	Italy	EMS	EMU (PY, M)	EMU (I)
1.0	4.15	4.14	4.16	4.15	4.15	4.15	4.17
2.0	4.09	4.06	4.12	4.09	4.09	4.09	4.21
3.0	3.97	3.93	4.02	3.98	3.97	3.97	4.31
4.0	3.81	3.76	3.87	3.82	3.81	3.82	4.45

Germany targets nominal income (or money). In this regime, all of the European countries get the German interest rate; that is, column 6 is the same as column 2. As expected (from the covariances with world output), French interest rates rise, while the Italian and British interest rates fall. However, the changes are quite small. Even at higher levels of risk aversion, the interest rates do not vary by more than 5 or 6 basis points. Column 7 gives the interest rates under EMU, with the European central bank targeting nominal income (or money). And as expected (since European output has virtually the same correlation with world output as does German output), this regime switch does not matter much; interest rates do not vary by more than a couple basis points. Column 8 shows what would happen if, instead, the European central bank targeted the nominal interest rate.[12] The choice of targeting procedure does matter. At higher levels of risk aversion, real interest rates vary by 50 or 60 basis points.

Table 4a tells a story that is very similar to the one in Table 3. Table 4a gives French and German equity prices when trend inflation is set equal to zero (and when velocity is set equal to one); these prices have been normalized to one under flexible rates to ease cross regime comparisons. The French stock market falls when the franc is pegged to the DM, because German output is more highly correlated with world output than

Table 4a. *French and German equity prices*

k	F	France EMS	EMU	F	Germany EMS	EMU
1.0	1.0000	0.9998	0.9999	1.0000	1.0000	1.0001
2.0	1.0000	0.9997	0.9998	1.0000	1.0000	1.0002
3.0	1.0000	0.9995	0.9997	1.0000	1.0000	1.0002
4.0	1.0000	0.9994	0.9996	1.0000	1.0000	1.0003

---

[12] See Canzoneri and Dellas (1995a) for a discussion of this targeting procedure. The reader will be able to derive the formula for the real interest rate in this case.

Table 4b. *French and German equity prices: effects of anticipated inflation*

	$V=1\ \Pi_{f,F}=1.06$ $\Pi_{g,F}=1.04=\Pi_{EMS}$ $\Pi_{EMU}=1.05\ k=2$			$V=2\ \Pi_{f,F}=1.06$ $\Pi_{g,F}=1.04=\Pi_{EMS}$ $\Pi_{EMU}=1.05\ k=2$			$V=2\ \Pi_{f,F}=1.07$ $\Pi_{g,F}=1.02=\Pi_{EMS}$ $\Pi_{EMU}=1.03\ k=2$		
	F	EMS	EMU	F	EMS	EMU	F	EMS	EMU
France	1.000	1.019	1.009	1.000	1.009	1.004	1.000	1.023	1.018
Germany	1.000	1.000	0.991	1.000	1.000	0.996	1.000	1.000	0.995

is French output and the risk premium rises. Then, the French stock market rises under EMU, because European output is (very marginally) less correlated with world output than is German output and the risk premium falls. But as in the case of real interest rates, the differences across regimes are very small. Even at higher levels of risk aversion, equity prices do not vary by much more than half a percent. The same thing happens in Italy and the U.K.; their stock markets move in the opposite direction of the French, but the revaluations are quite small.

The changes in trend inflation that seem to accompany regime switches have a more important effect on national stock markets than do risk premia. Table 4b reports three experiments. In the first, France and Germany start with trend inflations of 6% and 4%, respectively. In the EMS, France has to adopt Germany's inflation rate; in EMU, we assume the European central bank settles on the average, 5%. France's stock market rises about 2% on joining the EMS, and falls halfway back under EMU. These are very significant changes, considering that trend inflation rates have only changed a few percentage points.

This first experiment may overstate the impact of anticipated inflation on national stock markets, since it assumes that velocity is equal to one, and consequently that all sales are subject to the seignorage tax. It is difficult to say what fraction of sales should be subject to this tax. M1 aggregates would suggest velocities of about 4; broader aggregates give smaller velocities. In the second experiment, we have doubled velocity. Fluctuations in the equity prices are roughly halved. If we doubled velocity again, the fluctuations in equity prices would once again be roughly halved.

On the other hand, the first experiment may understate the importance of anticipated inflation, since the inflation differentials postulated are much smaller than what Europe has experienced over the last decade. The third experiment keeps velocity at two, and increases the differential in inflation rates. France starts with 7%, while Germany starts with 2%; in EMU, the European central bank settles on a trend rate of 3%. The

Table 4c. *French and German equity prices: effects of anticipated regime shift*

	$\Pi_{g,F} = 1.04$ $\Pi_{f,F} = 1.06$ $\Pi_{EMU} = 1.05$ $V = 2$ $k = 2$		$\Pi_g = 1.03 = \Pi_f$; then $\Pi_f = 1.07$ and $\Pi_g = 1.03$. $V = 2$ $k = 2$	
	EMU in 4	EMU in 10	Franc Fort	Floating in 1
France	1.000	0.999	1.000	0.978
Germany	1.000	1.001	1.000	1.000

French stock market rises 2.3% on pegging the franc to the DM, and falls back 0.5% as trend inflation goes up after EMU.

We have not tried to model the short-term credibility problems that might arise just before a regime change. However, our analysis does give some idea of their potential magnitude. A small "overnight" capital gain is equivalent to a huge annual return. So, even a relatively small expected capital gain or loss can lead to large international portfolio adjustments. We can use our model to calculate the magnitudes of the expected capital gains or losses that might be generated by various "news" events.

Table 4c gives two examples. In the first, France and Germany are in what we interpret as a flexible rate regime with trend inflations of 6% and 4%, respectively. EMU, with a trend inflation of 5%, is expected in four years. French and German equity prices are normalized to one on this scenario. Then, "news" leads investors to believe that EMU will be delayed for six years. The French stock market is immediately expected to fall by 0.1%, just because the 1% fall in French inflation is expected to be delayed by six years. In the second example, France has pegged the franc to the DM, and equity prices are normalized on the belief that the "franc fort" policy will continue indefinitely. Then, "news" causes investors to believe that the policy will be abandoned, and that trend inflation in France will increase by 4%. This generates an immediate expected capital loss of more than 2% on the French stock market. These examples show that "news" about relatively small changes in trend inflation can really destabilize world stock exchanges.

In Canzoneri and Dellas (1995b), we show that regime switches can also have a big impact on the stability of price levels and exchange rates. Moving from floating rates to the EMS, all of Europe adopts German price and exchange rate volatility. Moving from the EMS to EMU, price volatility is cut by a fifth, and exchange rate volatility is cut by a third. This is because European productivity is more stable than German productivity. Note, however, that this assumes the European central bank targets nominal income. If the European central bank were to switch money targeting, price and exchange rate volatility would approximately double.

This is due to the fact that velocity shocks are no longer automatically accommodated.

IV. Summary and Conclusions

The model outlined in Section II suggested that vacillations in monetary arrangements have two basic implications for the financial markets of Europe: (i) The risk premium on nominal assets depends on the correlation between the output driving the price level and the output driving consumption. If the correlation increases as we pass from one regime to another, then the (negative) correlation between the price level and consumption increases, raising the risk premium. The real interest rate rises and the stock market falls. (ii) Anticipated inflation lowers the value of equity in firms whose sales are denominated in that currency. A change in monetary regime that lowers anticipated inflation will raise the value of the stock market.

The model calibrations reported in Section III suggested which of these implications might be of some quantitative importance: (i) The correlations between price levels and consumption do vary from one regime to another, but the impact on risk premia appears to be negligible. Real interest rates did not vary more than a few basis points, and equity prices did not vary more than a few tenths of a percent. A switch in the central bank's targeting procedure had much more effect on the risk premium than any of the switches in international regime. (ii) The changes in anticipated inflation that may accompany a regime switch can have a very important impact on national stock markets. "News" about regime switches, and the associated trends in inflation, can be very destabilizing.

Our more specific conclusions for Europe are as follows: (i) Germany would seem to have relatively little to fear from EMU. The effect on risk premia is quite negligible, since the covariance between German output and world output is almost identical to the covariance between European output and world output. The chief danger lies in the effect on the German stock market, if Germany has to compromise on trend inflation. (ii) The stock markets in Italy, France or the U.K. would benefit significantly from any monetary arrangement that would lower the anticipated rate of inflation. (iii) Italy would benefit unambiguously from either a hard EMS or EMU. (iv) France's "franc fort" policy may benefit its stock market by keeping trend inflation low. (v) None of the countries would experience significant changes in real interest rates under any of the regime switches considered in this paper (unless central bank targeting procedures were also affected). (vi) "News" affecting expectations of inflation may be contributing directly to the current instability in national stock markets.

These are rather sweeping conclusions, and they must of course be qualified by the limitations of our model. The limitations are many. Some will be bothered by our assumption that velocity is exogenous; others will be bothered by the fact that velocity shocks have no effect on output or consumption. In future work, we hope to endogenize velocity and output by incorporating "liquidity" effects; it is hard to speculate how this modification might affect our conclusions. We can shed some light on the probable importance of two other simplifying assumptions. The representative agent paradigm, and its internationally "pooled equilibrium", causes some (including us) to wince. However, we have little reason to think that this simplification is driving our results here; Dellas (1995) considers a model with home (or non-traded) goods and comes to many of the same conclusions. Similarly, we doubt that the lack of price rigidities and endogenous output is important to our conclusions. In Canzoneri and Dellas (1995a), we compared a flexible price model with a "Fisher-Gray" contract model (in which nominal wages are fixed) and found that both produced similar risk premia.

References

Canzoneri, Matthew and Dellas, Harris: Real interest rates and central bank operating procedures. CEPR DP 1099, Jan. 1995a.

Canzoneri, Matthew and Dellas, Harris: Monetary integration in Europe: Implications for real interest rates, national stock markets and the volatility of prices and exchange rates. CEPR DP 1100, Jan. 1995b.

Dellas, Harris: European monetary integration: A new approach. Mimeo, 1995.

Glick, Reuven and Rogoff, Kenneth: Global versus country-specific produtivity shocks and the current account. Paper presented at the European Summer Symposium in Macroeconomics, Tarragona, 1993.

Goodfriend, Marvin and Small, David: *Operating Procedures and the Conduct of Monetary Policy: Conference Proceedings*. Finance and Economics Discussion Series, Federal Reserve Board, Mar. 1993.

Hansen, Lars and Singleton, Kenneth: Stochastic consumption, risk aversion and the temporal behavior of asset returns. *Journal of Political Economy 91* (2), 249–65, 1983.

Mankiw, Gregory and Zeldes, Stephen: The consumption of stockholders and nonstockholders. Mimeo, 1991.

McCallum, Bennett: Robustness Properties of a Rule for Monetary Policy. In Karl Brunner and Bennett McCallum (eds.), *Money, Cycles, and Exchange Rates: Essays in Honor of Allan H. Meltzer*, Carnegie-Rochester Conference Series on Public Policy 29, North-Holland, Amsterdam, 1988.

McKinnon, Ronald: The rules of the game: International money from a historical perspective. *Journal of Economics Literature 31*, 1–44, 1993.

Woodford, Michael: Currency competition and the transition to monetary union: Does competition between currencies lead to price level and exchange rate stability? In Alberto Giovannini and Colin Mayer (eds.), *European Financial Integration*, Cambridge University Press, 1991.

Exchange Rate versus Price Level Targets and Output Stability

*Asbjørn Rødseth**

University of Oslo, N-0317 Oslo, Norway

Abstract

Two alternative targets for monetary policy are considered: stability of the price level (or the rate of inflation) and stability of the exchange rate. The interest rate is the main instrument of the central bank. Credibility requires low output variability. The advantages of the alternative policy rules from the point of view of output stability are considered in the simplest possible model. Conditions favouring a price level rule are high volatility of aggregate demand, low volatility of aggregate supply, high volatility of the foreign price level, a low price elasticity of aggregate demand and a high price elasticity of aggregate supply.

I. Introduction

Which policy accords the greater stability in output: a price level target or an exchange rate target? If a price level target is chosen, how does output volatility depend on the weights given to home and foreign goods in the price index? These are the main questions addressed in this paper.

Assigning monetary policy to a single target is seldom the first-best optimal policy. However, attempts to do better by using more discretion can easily fail. The advantage of simple rules is their transparency. This makes it easier to establish credibility, and the public will make fewer expectational errors. It also promotes accountability, and may limit the scope for errors of judgement in the conduct of policy. However, if the effects of simple rules on output variability and other real variables are too harmful, sooner or later they will be discarded. Thus, low output variability also becomes a condition for the credibility of the policy in question.

In the literature on credibility, the main focus has been on the time-consistency problem; see Kydland and Prescott (1977) and Barro and Gordon (1983). As argued by McCallum (1995), this emphasis seems exaggerated. Every day society shows its ability to overcome the time-consistency problem in taxation, punishment of crime and other areas.

*I have benefited from discussions with Øistein Røisland, Arent Skjæveland and Birger Vikøren, and from comments by two anonymous referees. Financial support from the Norwegian Research Council is gratefully acknowledged.

Why this should be more difficult in monetary policy is not clear. The great deflations associated with resumption of the gold standard after World War I showed that central bankers and politicians are sometimes willing to adhere to a monetary rule even if it causes extreme hardship in the short run. Of course, we also see far too many examples of the opposite behaviour, where a sensible rule is bent by the same politicians who just enacted it as soon as a short-run gain is in sight. This kind of behaviour is clearly worth studying. However, our policy advice should not always be based on the idea that rule bending is unavoidable. Bad habits can be broken. If the authorities stick to a price level or an exchange rate rule long enough, the public will learn to expect this behaviour, and credibility will be established.

The literature on time consistency and credibility provides several suggestions for promoting credibility: central bank independence, statutory targets for monetary policy, "the conservative central banker" and incentive contracts for central bankers.[1] These devices may be used to support the rules we study, but they are neither necessary nor sufficient for credibility. Those who purport to solve the time-consistency problem in reality move it to another set of agents. In a democracy, a broad political consensus is an important condition for credibility. Such a consensus is difficult to achieve if the side-effects of a policy are too harmful. Thus, we are back to the situation where low output variability is important for credibility.[2]

The framework of analysis in the main part of the paper is as follows. A stationary environment free from autocorrelation is assumed. Thus, this period's expectations of the levels of all exogenous variables in the next period are constant. Wages are set before this period's realizations of the exogenous shocks are known. This means that aggregate supply responds positively to an increase in the price level. Aggregate demand depends on the real interest rate and on the real exchange rate. The output level and the price of home goods are determined by the intersection of supply and demand. The central bank sets the interest rate after the exogenous shocks have been realized. It adjusts the interest rate to achieve either price stability or a constant exchange rate, and it has full knowledge of the structure of the economy. Thus, its policy is always successful.

The policy is credible in the sense that expectations are based on the

---

[1] The efficiency of contracts which relate the pay of the governor to inflation performance may be questioned. The governorship of a central bank is a public office, not a salesman job. The authority of the governor may be endangered if his actions are perceived to be dictated by personal economic interests rather than by the public good.

[2] Credibility also depends on whether fiscal policy is consistent with the inflation or exchange rate target; see Sargent (1986).

notion that the central bank sticks to its target. As discussed above, it may be more difficult to establish credibility for some targets than for others. One way to find out is to assume *provisionally* that all alternatives can be made credible by consistent behaviour over time, and look at what variations in output the authorities must then put up with.

The central bank does not use foreign exchange intervention as a policy tool. The interpretation is that capital mobility is so high that interventions are of little use. It is this fact which makes it necessary for the central bank to choose between a price level target and an exchange rate target. If the central bank had two instruments at its disposal, it might attempt to reach both targets simultaneously.

Immediate predecessors of the present paper are Alogoskoufis (1994) and Genberg (1989) who study how the optimal choice of exchange rate regime depends on the nature of the disturbances hitting the economy. Useful surveys are also Marston (1985) and Argy (1990). Another related paper on targeting nominal income is Bean (1983). These studies belong to the tradition which started with the classical article by Poole (1970) on the choice of monetary policy instrument. I use the same methodology as in these earlier papers. The differences are that I consider a price level target as the guideline for monetary policy under flexible exchange rates, and that the interest rate is treated as the monetary policy instrument in all regimes. Some arguments for regarding the interest rate as the main instrument of monetary policy can be found in Goodhart (1994). In the earlier literature, flexible exchange rates usually meant a money supply target. The practice of targeting the pricel level is considered in Leiderman and Svensson (1995).

The model is kept as simple as possible in the belief that we need a thorough understanding of the simple case first. The conclusions also hold if there is trend growth in the real variables or in the price level target. The analysis of permanent shocks in Section VI shows that the main results can be generalized to a case with autocorrelation in the exogenous shocks. The next step is obviously to make the analysis more dynamic. One would like to allow for more persistence in inflation and output, for stock accumulation and for policy lags.[3]

The standard distinction between price level and inflation targets is not relevant in our context. A price level target specifies a time path for the price level. The time path may imply inflation. An inflation target specifies

---

[3] Røisland (1996) compares inflation targets and exchange rate targets when the interest rate affects the price of home goods with lags through a Phillips-curve mechanism. Lønning (1995) seeks a robust interest rate rule for hitting an inflation target when inflation responds with a lag.

a target inflation rate (possibly zero) to be applied no matter what the initial price level is. This distinction becomes relevant when the central bank misses its target. With an inflation target, the central bank should then forget about past misses and concentrate on achieving the target inflation rate in the future. With a price level target, the central bank should compensate for past misses by lower future inflation in order to bring the price level back to the preassigned path. In the simple model studied here the central bank always hits its target. Then inflation and price level targets are equivalent.

II. The Model

We look at a small country. As in the Mundell-Fleming models there are two commodities, one home good and one foreign good.

All variables (except the interest rate) are measured in logs and relative to their unconditional expectations. The short-run aggregate supply function is

$$y = \beta(p - w + u), \tag{1}$$

where y is output, p the price of home goods, w the (pre-determined) wage rate, u an exogenous labour augmenting productivity shock and β a positive constant.

Aggregate demand is given by

$$y = -\alpha[i - (Ep - p)] + \gamma(e + p_* - p) + v, \tag{2}$$

where i is the domestic nominal interest rate and Ep this period's expectation of next period's price level. Thus, $i - (Ep - p)$ is the *ex ante* real interest rate. e is the exchange rate and p_* the price of imported goods. The real exchange rate is then $e + p_* - p$. v is an exogenous demand shock, and α and γ are positive constants. Since there are no autocorrelation and no lags, Ep is the same as the unconditional expectation of p, and since we measure all variables relative to their expected values, Ep is zero. The real interest rate can thus be written $i + p$. A high price level this period means that we can expect a lower price level next period, and this raises the real interest rate. At this point the assumption of no autocorrelation in the shocks is critical.

The equilibrium condition for the foreign exchange market is

$$i = i_* + (Ee - e) + z = r_* + (Ep_* - p_*) + (Ee - e) + z, \tag{3}$$

which says that the domestic interest rate is equal to the foreign interest rate, i_*, plus the expected rate of depreciation, $Ee - e$, and a stochastic risk premium, z. Ee is the exchange rate expected this period to prevail next period. The foreign nominal interest rate is equal to the foreign real interest rate, r_*, plus the expected foreign rate of inflation, $Ep_* - p_*$. Because there is no autocorrelation, and because of the way e and p_* are measured, $Ee = Ep_* = 0$. This means that if we have a depreciated exchange rate today, it is expected to appreciate next period. If capital mobility is perfect, z is always zero. The model does not require perfect capital mobility, but the central bank must not intervene by buying or selling foreign currency. An alternative interpretation of z is that it represents credibility shocks which are unrelated to the state of the economy, e.g. political events.

A fixed exchange rate means that $e = 0$ always. A price level target has to be defined relative to some price index. Let the consumer price index be $q = a'p + (1-a')(e+p_*)$, where a' is the weight on home goods. Targeting the consumer price index means setting $q = 0$. More generally, we can write the policy target as

$$ap + (1-a)(e+bp_*) = 0, \tag{4}$$

where a and b are parameters which define the target. This formulation encompasses both a fixed exchange rate ($a = b = 0$) and alternative price level targets ($0 \leq a \leq 1$, $b = 1$). Since the purpose of setting a target is to preserve some degree of nominal stability, we only consider rules where $0 \leq a \leq 1$ and $0 \leq b \leq 1$.

Equations (1)–(4) determine the four endogenous variables y, p, e and i. The exogenous stochastic shocks are w, u, v, r_*, z and p_*.

III. Solution

Since the model is linear, it is straightforward to solve for endogenous variables as functions of the shocks. One way of proceeding is to form an aggregate demand curve relating y and p by combining equations (2), (3) and (4) and eliminating i and e. Then we combine this curve with the aggregate supply curve (1) in order to find y and p.

The policy target (4) can be rewritten with e on the l.h.s. as

$$e = -bp_* - \frac{a}{1-a}p. \tag{5}$$

By inserting this in the interest parity condition (3), we get the central bank reaction function

$$i = r_* + Ep_* + Ee + z - (1-b)p_* + \frac{a}{1-a}p. \tag{6}$$

The aggregate demand curve is found by substituting (5) and (6) in (2). This gives

$$y = -\frac{\alpha+\gamma}{1-a}p - \alpha(r_*+z) - \alpha E(p_*+e-p) + (1-b)(\alpha+\gamma)p_* + v. \tag{7}$$

Since we are now looking at shocks that are uncorrelated over time, $E(p_*+e-p) = 0$. The reason why the expected real exchange rate next period is kept in the equation is that we need it in Section VI where we study permanent shocks. Aggregate demand is a declining function of p, r_* and z, as should be expected. If we have a price level target, $b = 1$ and a foreign nominal shock (p_*) has no effect. If the exchange rate is fixed $(b = 0)$, an increase in p_* raises the demand for home goods. There are two reasons for this. One is that an increase in p_* raises the real exchange rate. The other is that an increase in p_* reduces the interest rate, i, as can be seen from the central bank reaction function (6).

The aggregate demand curve (7) is illustrated in Figure 1 along with the supply curve (1) (S). Alternative targets for monetary policy change the shape of the demand curve, while they leave the supply curve unaffected. The price elasticity of aggregate demand in (7) is inversely proportional to $1-a$. Thus, the higher the weight on home goods in the policy target, the more elastic the aggregate demand. A fixed exchange rate $(a = 0)$ always gives the lowest demand elasticity. In Figure 1 a price level target always means a flatter demand curve than an exchange rate target. Thus, the

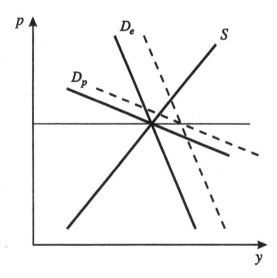

Fig. 1.

demand curve marked D_e is for an exchange rate target, while D_p is for a price level target. While a changes the price elasticity of aggregate demand, and nothing else, b only determines the effect of an imported inflation shock on aggregate demand.

By equating aggregate supply and demand, (1) and (7), we find (assuming $a \neq 1$ and $E(p_* + e - p) = 0$ the equilibrium values:

$$p = \mu[-\alpha(r_* + z) + (1-b)(\alpha + \gamma)p_* + v + \beta(w-u)] \tag{8}$$

$$y = \beta\mu\left[-\alpha(r_* + z) + (1-b)(\alpha + \gamma)p_* + v - \frac{\alpha + \gamma}{1-a}(w-u)\right] \tag{9}$$

where

$$\mu = \frac{1}{\beta + (\alpha + \gamma)/(1-a)} = \frac{1-a}{(1-a)\beta + (\alpha + \gamma)}$$

is the inverse of the sum of the price elasticities of demand and supply.
When the solution for p is inserted in (5) and (6), we find that:

$$e = -p_* + \mu\left[\frac{a}{1-a}[\alpha(r_* + z) - v - \beta(w-u)] + (1-b)(\beta + \alpha + \gamma)p_*\right] \tag{10}$$

$$i = \frac{(1-a)(\beta + \alpha) + \gamma}{(1-a)\beta + \alpha + \gamma}(r_* + z)$$

$$+ \mu\left[\frac{a}{1-a}[v + \beta(w-u)] - (1-b)(\beta + \alpha + \gamma)p_*\right]. \tag{11}$$

Note that if the exchange rate is fixed ($a = 0$, $b = 0$), the solutions for e and i come out as $e = 0$ and $i = r_* - p_* + z = i_* + z$, as they should. Note also that the unconditional expectations of p, y, e and i are all zero in accordance with our assumptions. Furthermore, the solution of the model for $a = 1$ is the same as the limiting form of (8)–(11) as a approaches 1. In particular, $a = 1$ yields $p = 0$ and $y = \beta(u - w)$.

IV. The Effects of Shocks

Depending on the origin of the shocks, we distinguish between demand shocks (v, r_*, z and p_*) and supply shocks (u and w).

Demand Shocks

The four variables v, r_*, z and p_* all shift the aggregate demand curve, while they leave the aggregate supply curve unchanged. One may regard v as representing a genuine demand shock, r_* and z as foreign exchange shocks and p_* as an imported nominal shock. While an increase in v raises aggregate demand directly, an increase in r_* or z raises the domestic interest rate and, thus, reduces demand indirectly. As already explained, p_* has no effect on aggregate demand if $b = 1$; i.e., if there is a price level rule. If $0 \leq b < 1$, an increase in p_* has a positive effect on aggregate demand because it leads to a real depreciation and a reduced interest rate.

The effect of an increase in v is shown in Figure 1. The demand curve shifts to the right. Measured horizontally, the size of the shift is independent of the monetary target. The flatter the demand curve, the weaker the effect on both output and the price of home goods. Relative to an exchange rate target, a price level target reduces the effects of demand shocks on p and y. The higher the weight on home goods (a), the more subdued the response.

The reason for the damped effect can be seen from (11). When $a > 0$, a positive demand shock induces the central bank to increase the interest rate. This in turn leads to an appreciation, as can be seen from (10). A higher interest rate and an appreciation both have a negative effect on aggregate demand. The effects of other demand shocks are similar, except that imported nominal shocks have no effect when there is a price level rule.

The output effects of demand shocks can be neutralized completely if one sets $a = 1$; i.e., if the central bank stabilizes producer prices. In this case a positive demand shock induces a fall in the consumer price index since the exchange rate appreciates and foreign goods become less expensive. A fall in the consumer price index will be the result whenever $a > a'$.

If $0 \leq a < 1$, a high supply elasticity β increases the output effect of a genuine demand shock, while high demand elasticities α and γ reduce it. Foreign exchange shocks produce stronger output effects the higher α is.

Supply Shocks

An increase in u or a decrease in w shifts the supply curve to the right, as illustrated in Figure 2. The shift is, of course, the same regardless of monetary target. The output effect is strongest when the demand curve is relatively flat. Relative to an exchange rate target, a price level target increases the effect of a supply shock on y and reduces the effect on p. The

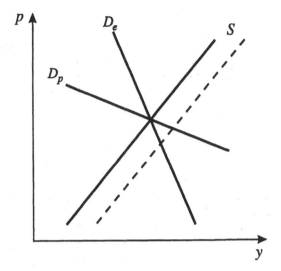

Fig. 2.

greater the weight on home goods (*a*), the stronger the output response and the smaller the price response.

When there is a price level target, the central bank responds to a positive supply shock by lowering its interest rate to stimulate demand and thereby stabilize the price level; cf. (11). This reduction in the interest rate induces the depreciation that can be seen in (10), and which also stimulates demand.

High price elasticities in demand and supply increase the effect of supply shocks on output. High price elasticities combined with a high weight on home goods, *a*, produce the strongest output effects of supply shocks.

Exchange Rate Volatility

When a price level rule is in operation, an increase in domestic producer prices, *p*, has to be offset by an appreciation and vice versa. This follows directly from (4). As a consequence, a price level target may produce a high volatility of both the real and the nominal exchange rate. As can be seen from (10), a high *a* increases the response of the nominal exchange rate to all kinds of shocks except p_*. The same can be shown to hold for the real exchange rate by combining (8) and (10). This may throw some light on the increased volatility of exchange rates which followed the transition to floating in the 1970s.

If β is high and there are strong supply shocks, a price level rule may produce particularly strong exchange rate volatility. A high β means that the short-run marginal cost of production is fairly constant, and that the supply curve is relatively flat. Monetary policy, which works through aggregate demand, is then unable to have much effect on p. A negative supply shock must then be balanced by a large reduction in import prices, and this requires a large appreciation. The effects on the real exchange rate will be even stronger, since p and e move in opposite directions.

V. The Optimal Policy Rule

We start this section by looking for the level of a which minimizes the variance of y, given that we have a price level rule. In general the authorities will also be concerned with the variance of the price level. However, the desire for price stability is already taken care of when a price level rule is implemented. It may be argued that this is sufficient, and that the choice of exactly which price index to stabilize can then be based on other arguments, e.g. the variance of y. Later on in this section we look briefly at how the optimum is modified when special importance is attached to a low variance of the consumer price index, although it is far from obvious that this should be more important than stabilizing the producer price index or the import price index. In between we argue that some variation in output may be desirable, and take a brief look at how this changes the optimal a. At the end we examine the optimal level of b and the question of fixed versus flexible rates.

It is convenient to define two aggregates which summarize the demand and supply shocks:

$$d = -\alpha(r_* + z) + (1 - b)(\alpha + \gamma)p_* + v$$

$$s = \beta(-w + u).$$

These are measured in the same unit as output. Throughout this section we assume that d and s are independent stochastic variables.

Equation (9) can be rewritten as

$$y = xd + (1 - x)s \quad \text{where} \quad x = \frac{\beta(1 - a)}{\beta(1 - a) + (\alpha + \gamma)}. \tag{12}$$

Since there is a unique correspondence between x and a, finding the optimal a is the same as finding the optimal x.

Let the variances of d and s be σ_d and σ_s, respectively. From (12) the variance of output is then

$$\sigma_y = x^2\sigma_d + (1 - x)^2\sigma_s. \tag{13}$$

Note that a enters the objective function only through x, while b enters only through σ_d. This shows that we can first choose the optimal b by minimizing σ_d and then the optimal a. For the moment we just take the level of b as given, possibly equal to some optimum, possibly equal to one.

The first-order condition for minimum σ_y is

$$\frac{d\sigma_y}{dx} = 2x\sigma_d - 2(1-x)\sigma_s = 0.$$

The second-order condition is always satisfied. By solving the first-order condition we find that the optimal weight on demand shocks is $x = \sigma_s/(\sigma_d + \sigma_s)$. From the definition of x this can be translated into the optimal weights on foreign goods in the price level target:

$$1 - a = \frac{\alpha + \gamma}{\beta} \frac{\sigma_s}{\sigma_d}. \tag{14}$$

The more volatile supply is relative to demand, the higher the optimal weight on foreign goods. The term $(\alpha + \gamma)/\beta$ is the ratio between the price elasticities of demand and supply. *Ceteris paribus*, a higher level of this ratio means a higher optimal weight on foreign goods. The reason is that when the price elasticity on one side of the market is high, a shock originating on the other side of the market has a large effect on output.

The *ceteris paribus* clause is needed because the original impact of the shocks, and thus σ_d and σ_s, are not independent of the price elasticities. This is obvious from the definitions of d and s. As an example, assume that the shocks v, r_*, z, u and w are all independent. Also assume that $b = 1$. We then need not be concerned about p_*. Denoting variances the same way as before, the optimal weight on foreign goods can be written

$$1 - a = (\alpha + \gamma)\beta \frac{\sigma_u + \sigma_w}{\alpha^2(\sigma_{r*} + \sigma_z) + \sigma_v}. \tag{15}$$

In this case the overall effect of an increase in the supply elasticity β is to increase, not decrease, the optimal weight on foreign goods. The overall effect of a higher α is ambiguous when we take account of its impact on σ_d. However, σ_d is independent of γ and, thus, a higher elasticity of demand with respect to the real exchange rate unambiguously increases the optimal weight on foreign goods.

Obviously, these conclusions are not robust to small changes in the way the shocks enter the model, e.g. whether the productivity shock is labour augmenting or neutral. One should therefore be content with the conclusion that *the optimal weight on foreign goods is higher, the higher the volatility of supply relative to demand, and the higher the price elasticity of demand relative to supply, recalling that particular parameters may impinge on both these ratios.*

Since the r.h.s. in (14) is always positive, the optimal a is always smaller than one. It is never optimal to stabilize the producer price index. There is nothing in (14) to prevent a from being negative, however. This happens if aggregate supply is sufficiently volatile in comparison with demand. Since we require $0 \le a \le 1$, a negative value for a from (14) means that the actual optimum is a corner solution with $a = 0$; i.e., the central bank should target the price of imports. If the volatility of p_* is small, we may as well choose a fixed exchange rate.

So far we have assumed that minimum output variability is desirable. However, even if wages are fully flexible, real shocks (u, v, z or r_*) may have output effects through two channels. First, for a given level of employment, a shock has a direct productivity effect on output. Second, real shocks change the wedge between consumer and producer real wages, and this may change labour supply. Following Aizenman and Frenkel (1986) the optimal output level may be defined as that which would prevail if the nominal wage were fully flexible. However, disequilibrium variations in employment are not the same as equilibrium variations. The distribution of employment among individuals is likely to be different and less desirable. Changing one's labour supply as a response to a change in the real wage is not the same as being laid-off or called in for compulsory overtime. Here we circumvent the problem by assuming that labour supply is inelastic, and that the only desired variation in output is the direct effect of productivity shocks for a given level of employment.

If labour supply is constant, the aggregate supply function with flexible wages is[4]

$$y = \frac{\beta}{1+\beta} u. \tag{16}$$

If this is our benchmark, the criterion for choosing the monetary target is to minimize $\sigma = E[y - (\beta/(1+\beta))u]^2$. By the same procedure as above (and retaining the assumption of independent shocks and $b = 1$) we get the optimal weight on foreign goods:

$$1 - a = (\alpha + \gamma)\beta \frac{\sigma_u + \sigma_w - (1/(1+\beta))\sigma_u}{\sigma_d + (\beta^2/(1+\beta))\sigma_u}. \tag{17}$$

---

[4]Suppose the aggregate production function is $y = \theta(n+u)$, where n is the deviation of employment from its expected value and θ is the elasticity of output with respect to the input of labour. Then profit maximization yields an aggregate supply function $y = (\theta/(1-\theta))(p - w + u)$. Thus, the price elasticity of supply is $\beta = \theta/(1-\theta)$. This means that $\theta = \beta/(1+\beta)$, and that the production function can be written as $y = (\beta/(1+\beta))(n+u)$.

Compared to (15), the numerator has been reduced and the denominator increased. The optimal weight on foreign goods is thus reduced. Naturally, making a limited output effect of productivity shocks desirable has the same effect on the optimal weight as reducing the variance of productivity. However, the optimal weight on foreign goods is still positive, and the remarks above about the effects of different parameters still hold. The only exception is that it is no longer certain that an increase in σ_u raises the optimal weight on the prices of foreign goods. If σ_w is large relative to σ_d, the result may be the opposite.

We now turn to the case where it is of particular interest to stabilize the consumer price index. Suppose we want to minimize a weighted average $\sigma = \lambda \sigma_q + (1-\lambda) \sigma_y$, where σ_q is the variance of consumer prices, $q = a'p + (1-a')(e+p_*)$, and $0 < \lambda < 1$. Of course σ_q is minimized by setting $a = a'$. Denote by a'' the weight on home goods obtained in (14) by minimizing σ_y. It is then no surprise to find that if we minimize a weighted average of the two variances, the outcome is a weighted average of a' and a'':

$$a = \omega a' + (1-\omega)a'' \tag{18}$$

where

$$\omega = \frac{\lambda[\beta(1-a')+(\alpha+\gamma)](\sigma_d+\sigma_s)}{\lambda[\beta(1-a')+(\alpha+\gamma)](\sigma_d+\sigma_s)+(1-\lambda)\beta^2(\alpha+\gamma)\sigma_d}.$$

Clearly $0 < \omega < 1$. The higher λ is, the higher the weight on a' relative to a''. If (18) yields a negative a, then we have the corner solution $a = 0$.

From (14) it is seen that a'' does not depend on a'.[5] Whether a'' is smaller than or greater than a' depends only on the relative importance of supply and demand shocks. The more weight we assign to stabilizing consumer prices, the closer the optimal a is to a'. The relationship between the other parameters and the optimal a is complicated, because they affect ω and a'' simultaneously. However, the optimal a is still increasing in σ_d and decreasing in σ_s. It is always less than one, and may be zero if aggregate supply is sufficiently volatile.

As regards the choice of b, if the foreign nominal shock is uncorrelated with all the other shocks, the optimum is obviously $b = 1$. Stabilizing import prices is then always preferable to stabilizing the exchange rate, unless the foreign price level is perfectly predictable. However, there are reasons to believe that p_* and r_* are correlated. Exactly how depends on

---

[5] The actual consumption share of foreign goods may have an indirect effect through the price elasticity γ.

the monetary policy of the rest of the world and on the shocks that hit there. The demand shock v could also represent the effect of foreign income on the demand for our home goods, and must then be expected to be correlated with p_* and r_*. For simplicity we assume away any correlation between p_* and z.

The variance of the aggregate demand shock is by definition

$$\sigma_d = E[-\alpha(r_* + z) + (1-b)(\alpha+\gamma)p_* + v]^2. \tag{19}$$

If we compute the first-order condition for a minimum with respect to b and solve it, we find:

$$b = 1 + \frac{Ep_*v - \alpha Ep_*r_*}{(\alpha+\gamma)Ep_*^2}. \tag{20}$$

Suppose the main driving force behind the disturbances from abroad are monetary shocks. Then a high foreign price level is likely to be accompanied by low foreign real interest rates and high foreign aggregate demand, the latter spilling over to the domestic economy also through v. This means that $Ep_*v > 0$ and $Ep_*r_* < 0$. Equation (20) then gives us a b greater than 1, and we should choose the corner solution $b = 1$. However, real shocks abroad may produce a pattern where a high income level and a high price level are connected with a *high* real interest rate. Then $Ep_*r_* > 0$, and b in (20) may be smaller than one, or even negative.

Note that if there is no uncertainty in p_*, the optimal b is indeterminate. If the foreign price level is perfectly predictable, it does not matter what weight we attach to it. If we confine b to the interval between zero and one, and the variance of p_* is low, it does not matter much for output variability which value of b we choose. On the other hand, a high variance of p_* would normally imply that the optimal b from the point of view of output stability is close to one.

For reasons of credibility and accountability, the actual choice may be between stabilizing a well-known price index and stabilizing the exchange rate. The choice could be between stabilizing the producer price index ($a = 1$, $b = 1$), the consumer price index ($a = a'$, $b = 1$), the import price index ($a = 0$, $b = 1$) or the exchange rate ($a = 0$, $b = 0$).

From the preceding analysis one can then conclude that a high volatility of aggregate demand relative to aggregate supply speaks for a high a; i.e., for targeting the producer price index rather than the consumer price index, and for targeting the consumer price index rather than the import price index. Similarly, a high price elasticity of demand relative to supply speaks for targeting the consumer price index rather than the producer price index, and the import price index rather than the consumer price index.

Favourable circumstances for targeting the exchange rate are the same as those which are favourable for targeting the import price index: a high volatility of supply relative to demand and high price elasticities of demand relative to supply. In addition, low volatility of the foreign price level is required. Exchange rate targeting obviously makes sense only if the exchange rate is fixed to a currency with a low variance of inflation. A positive correlation between the foreign price level and foreign real interest rate would be an extra argument in favour of targeting the exchange rate.

VI. Permanent Shocks

The model can easily be adapted to handle permanent shocks if we assume that the wage rate expected in the next period is equal to the wage rate which equates expected supply and demand for labour. This assumption excludes permanent wage shocks, but allows permanent shocks to the other variables. For simplicity we assume an exogenous supply of labour.

When shocks are permanent, we can no longer assume that $Ep = Ee = Ep_* = 0$. We have to go back to equation (7) to take into account the connection between aggregate demand and the real exchange rate expected in the next period. When there is an expected real depreciation, this increases the real interest rate and reduces aggregate demand.

We now need to find out how the expected real depreciation depends on the shocks. Suppose the shocks we look at happen in period 1. In period 2 wages are flexible, and a full equilibrium is expected to prevail. From then on all variables are expected to be constant. The expected aggregate demand in period 2 is then, cf. (2) and (3):

$$Ey = -\alpha(r_* + z) + \gamma E(e + p_* - p) + v, \tag{21}$$

where r_*, z and v are the shocks from period 1. Since we assume that the expected wage level is the one which makes expected labour demand equal to labour supply, the expected aggregate supply in period 2 is

$$Ey = \frac{\beta}{1+\beta} u, \tag{22}$$

where u is again the value of the shock in period 1; cf. (16). The expected real depreciation is found by equating expected supply and demand for home goods, (21) and (22). This yields

$$E(e + p_* - p) = \frac{\alpha}{\gamma}(r_* + z) - \frac{1}{\gamma} v + \frac{1}{\gamma} \frac{\beta}{1+\beta} u. \tag{23}$$

A positive shock to the demand for home goods requires a permanent real appreciation; a positive productivity shock requires a permanent real depreciation.

If we insert from (23) in (7), we get a new aggregate demand curve for period 1:

$$y = -\frac{\alpha+\gamma}{1-a}p - \alpha\left(1+\frac{\alpha}{\gamma}\right)(r_* + z) + (\alpha+\gamma)(1-b)p_*$$

$$+\left(1+\frac{\alpha}{\gamma}\right)v - \frac{\alpha}{\gamma}\frac{\beta}{1+\beta}u. \tag{24}$$

When this is compared to the demand curve with transitory shocks, there are three points to note:

(i) The price elasticity of aggregate demand is unaffected by the nature of the shocks. This also holds for the elasticity with respect to the foreign price level, p_*.

(ii) Demand shocks (r_*, z, v) of a given size have greater impact on this period's demand for home goods when they are permanent. The reason is the real interest rate effect. After a positive demand shock a real appreciation is expected, and this means a lower real interest rate now.

(iii) A permanent productivity shock has a direct impact on aggregate demand. One reason is the real interest rate effect which is represented in (24) by the last term. Another reason is that a permanent productivity shock raises permanent income. The impact of this on the demand for home goods can be represented by an increase in v which is equal to the fraction spent on home goods times the permanent increase in output, $(\beta/(1+\beta))u$. In spite of the negative interest rate effect, the overall impact on aggregate demand in (24) is positive if the fraction spent on home goods is not too small.

Since the slopes of the demand curves are not affected by the nature of the shocks, it is still true that a price level rule is better at dampening the output effect of demand shocks, and that an exchange rate rule is better at dampening the output effect of a shift in the supply curve. There is the added complication that a permanent productivity shock affects both supply and demand. In the normal case, when the shift in the demand curve is in the same direction as and smaller than the shift in the supply curve, a fixed exchange rate is still the best response to a productivity shock. However, the choice of policy rule matters less than if the demand curve had been unaffected.

VII. Concluding Comments

We started by asking: Which policy accords the greater stability in output: a price level target or an exchange rate target? From our study of the impact of various shocks we can conclude that:

(i) supply shocks have a stronger effect on output when the central bank pursues a price level target;

(ii) demand shocks have a stronger effect on output when the central bank pursues an exchange rate target; and

(iii) pure nominal shocks from abroad have a positive demand effect when the exchange rate is fixed but no real effect when there is a price level target.

A fixed exchange rate makes sense only if the foreign price level is relatively stable. Then it is not of great importance whether one stabilizes the exchange rate or import prices. Unless there is a strong negative correlation between the foreign price level and the foreign real interest rate, stabilizing import prices gives less output volatility than a fixed exchange rate. Whether there should also be a positive weight on home goods in the price index which is stabilized depends on the relative volatility of demand and supply shocks. Thus, the circumstances which would indicate a high weight on home goods are: (i) a high volatility of demand shocks; (ii) a low volatility of supply shocks;[6] (iii) a low price elasticity of aggregate demand; and (iv) a high price elasticity of aggregate supply. When applying these conclusions, one should be aware that the same underlying parameters may take part in determining both the price elasticities and the aggregate volatility of supply and demand.

As long as there is some supply-side uncertainty, it is never optimal to target producer prices. If the volatility of supply is high relative to the volatility of demand, and if the price elasticity of aggregate supply is high, it may be better to target the price of imports than to target any price index which has a positive weight on home goods.

In practice the choice may be between targeting the consumer price index and targeting the exchange rate. Then, the circumstances we just listed as favouring a high weight on the price of home goods will also favour targeting the consumer price index.

One side-effect of targeting a price index is high real exchange rate volatility. The real (and nominal) exchange rate volatility will be higher, the higher the weight on home goods in the price level target. It will be

---

[6] With a possible exception if it is desirable that supply shocks are reflected in output to some extent; see Section V.

particularly high if the short-run aggregate supply curve is relatively flat and there are strong supply shocks. This points to a potential problem with a price level rule in economies where there is more than one production sector. High volatility in the real exchange rate may mean that there have to be large and frequent redistributions of employment between sectors which produce mainly for the domestic and mainly for the foreign market.

As the remarks on credibility in the introduction indicated, a low variability of output and of the real exchange rate can both be expected to promote credibility.

Rødseth (1996) shows that stabilizing the quantity of money may be preferable to stabilizing the price level, but only if the demand function for money is stable (low volatility of money demand shocks) and the interest elasticity of the demand for money is not too high. A money supply target always reduces the output effect of supply shocks relative to a price level target. If the interest rate elasticity of money demand is not too high, it also dampens the output effect of demand shocks.

The relative volatility of supply and demand may depend on fiscal policy. Automatic fiscal stabilizers as well as active stabilization by fiscal means reduce the volatility of aggregate demand from our point of view. This speaks in favour of targeting the exchange rate or the domestic currency prices of foreign goods.

In reality there is always a lag from a change in the interest rate to its final effect on the price level. On the other hand, the interest rate has an immediate effect on the exchange rate. Because of this, our analysis may have been biased in favour of price level targets, since we assume a degree of success for that policy which is hardly attainable in practice. However, if foreign exchange shocks are large, immediate control of the exchange rate may require unacceptable swings in the interest rate. With high capital mobility and less than total credibility, a realistic fixed rate policy may have to allow short-run deviations from the target and a gradual approach towards it.

References

Aizenman, Joshua and Frenkel, Jacob A.: Targeting rules for monetary policy. *Economics Letters 21*, 183–87, 1986.
Alogoskoufis, George: On inflation, unemployment and the optimal exchange rate regime. In F. van der Ploeg (ed.), *Handbook of International Macroeconomics*, Blackwell, Oxford, 1994.
Argy, Victor: Choice of exchange rate regime for a smaller economy: A survey of some key issues. In V. Argy and P. D. Grauwe (eds.), *Choosing an Exchange Rate Regime: The Challenge for Smaller Industrial Countries*, International Monetary Fund, Washington, DC, 1990.

Barro, Robert J. and Gordon, David B.: Rules, discretion and reputation in a model of monetary policy. *Journal of Monetary Economics 12*, 101–21, 1983.

Bean, Charles R.: Targeting nominal income: An appraisal. *Economic Journal 93*, 806–19, 1983.

Genberg, Hans: Exchange rate management and macroeconomic policy: A national perspective. *Scandinavian Journal of Economics 91*, 439–69, 1989.

Goodhart, Charles A. E.: What should central banks do? What should be their macroeconomic objectives and operations? *Economic Journal 104*, 1424–36, 1994.

Kydland, Finn E. and Prescott, Edward C.: Rules rather than discretion: The inconsistency of optimal plans. *Journal of Political Economy 85*, 619–37, 1977.

Leiderman, Leonardo and Svensson, Lars E. O. (eds.): *Inflation Targets*. Centre for Economic Policy Research, London, 1995.

Lønning, Ingunn M.: Stabilizing inflation through interest rate policy: Searching for robust monetary policy rules. Memorandum 22, Department of Economics, University of Oslo, 1995.

Marston, Richard C.: Stabilization policies in open economies. In R. W. Jones and P. B. Kenen (eds.), *Handbook of International Economics*, North-Holland, Amsterdam, 1985.

McCallum, Bennett T.: Two fallacies concerning central-bank independence. *American Economic Review 85*, 207–11, 1995.

Poole, William: Optimal choice of monetary policy instrument in a simple stochastic macromodel. *Quarterly Journal of Economics 100*, 1169–90, 1970.

Rødseth, Asbjørn: Exchange rate versus price level targets. Memorandum 7, Department of Economics, University of Oslo, 1996.

Røisland, Øistein: The dynamic effects of exchange rate and price stabilization targets. Memorandum 9, Department of Economics, University of Oslo, 1996.

Sargent, Thomas J.: *Rational Expectations and Inflation.* Harper & Row, New York, 1986.

Does Financial Deregulation Cause a Consumption Boom?*

Jonas Agell and Lennart Berg

Uppsala University, S-751 20 Uppsala, Sweden

Abstract

According to a growing number of critics, the process of financial liberalisation in the 1980s is to blame for the volatile macroeconomic development in a number of countries, including the U.K. and the Nordic economies. We examine how financial deregulation affected one important component of aggregate demand, private consumption. A main finding is that the Swedish consumption boom of the late 1980s can be explained along other lines than financial deregulation. The mid-1980s also constituted a period when real wage growth picked up, and our data are consistent with the simple idea that permanent income dynamics was an important factor.

I. Introduction

The 1980s saw widespread financial liberalisation in many industrial countries, and a pronounced boom-to-bust cycle in some of them, including the U.K. and the Nordic countries.[1] A question of great interest for academics and policymakers is whether financial deregulation has contributed to the macroeconomic imbalances. According to a growing number of critical voices, the efficiency gains promised by the proponents of financial deregulation were swamped by macroeconomic transition costs. In this paper we try to make some headway on how financial liberalisation affected one important component of aggregate demand, namely private consumption. While we confine our attention to the Swedish case, we believe that the analysis has broader ramifications.

On November 21, 1985, the Board of the Swedish Riksbank abolished all ceilings on loans from banks and finance companies. Five years later, the Swedish economy was ripe for the most severe economic downturn since the early 1930s. Between 1991 and 1993, GDP and private consumption decreased dramatically, and open unemployment rose from a handsome 1.6 percent to an ominous 8.2 percent. At the same time asset prices

* We have benefited from presenting this paper at the Industrial Institute for Economic and Social Research, Stockholm School of Economics, the Swedish Riksbank and Uppsala University. We wish to thank Guglielmo Weber and two anonymous referees for useful comments.

[1] For a discussion of the Nordic experience, see Berg (1994).

tumbled, the banking system was on the verge of a systemic collapse, and the government deficit skyrocketed. Is there a connection?

According to many prominent observers, the answer is yes. The so-called 'November revolution' of the Riksbank fuelled the consumption boom of the late 1980s, and the associated rapid build-up of household debt had dire consequences when the economy started to slow down around 1990. A combination of adverse and interacting shocks — including the major tax reform of 1990–91, a severe international recession, and an exchange rate policy that tried to maintain a fixed exchange rate until the fall of 1992 — triggered a classical process of debt deflation. As financially vulnerable households tried to scale down indebtedness, consumption and asset prices fell in tandem.

Sometimes truth changes swiftly. At the time, an important argument, admittedly not substantiated by deeper analysis, in favour of lifting the regulations of credit markets was that they had lost their bite anyway. Due to easy access to mortgage financing (coupled with very high maximum loan-to-value ratios), borrowing within families, and the emergence of a variety of financial intermediaries operating outside the traditional banking system, Swedish consumers could supposedly circumvent much of the regulative network. Hence, the deregulation of financial markets was interpreted as a quite undramatic *de facto* acknowledgement of past financial developments.[2]

Two studies suggest that this argument represents more than a dangerous example of wishful thinking. Jappelli and Pagano (1989) use an Euler equation approach to test for credit rationing. Their results suggest that the first-order condition for intertemporal consumer optimisation in the absence of liquidity constraints is violated in most countries, in the sense that current disposable income helps to explain consumption. Sweden, however, stands out as an exception; although the data cover a period when financial regulations were largely intact, there is no sign of credit rationing. Campbell and Mankiw (1991) also apply an Euler equation approach to time-series data for several countries, but unlike Jappelli and Pagano they also focus on developments over time. While their evidence is consistent with a significant, but still fairly small, rationing effect in Sweden, they find no detectable decline in liquidity constraints over time.

In this paper we argue that much of the Swedish consumption boom of the late 1980s can indeed be attributed to other factors than the liberalisation of financial markets. The widespread belief that deregulation effects caused the sharp fall in personal savings between 1986–88 rests on the

---

[2] See Jonung (1993) for a discussion of the views of leading officials at the Riksbank around the mid-1980s.

simple observation that consumption growth was unusually brisk in the years immediately after the liberalisation of financial markets.[3] But what is often forgotten is that other important time series also turned around at the same time. Due to a recession, followed by a large devaluation in 1982, real per capita wage income (net of taxes and transfers) declined by 8.3 percent in the period 1980–83. Over the next three years, when exports led an economic recovery, real wage income grew by 8.7 percent.

Why should a wage boom spur consumption? The first possibility focuses on the implications from the life-cycle/permanent-income model that consumption ought to increase in periods when households make an upward revision of their expectations of future labour income. If the wage hikes in the mid-1980s affected the permanent-income perceptions of consumers who were unconstrained in credit markets, a consumption boom is the natural outcome. To the extent that permanent income increased relative to current income, borrowing would also increase. The second possibility is even simpler. If the consumption of a substantial minority of households closely tracks their wage income — because of liquidity constraints or rule-of-thumb behaviour — current wage growth ought to be contemporaneously correlated with consumption growth. While we do not rule out the possibility that financial liberalisation also played some role, we argue that either of these mechanisms may in fact explain the major part of the Swedish consumption boom.

The idea that consumption behaviour has in fact changed because of financial deregulation has been proposed in a number of papers; cf. Muellbauer and Murphy (1990), Miles (1992), Koskela, Loikkanen and Virén (1992) and Bayoumi (1993a). A common theme in these papers, focusing on other countries than Sweden, is that financial liberalisation may have had a direct effect on the consumption choices of previously credit constrained households, as well as an indirect effect operating via wealth effects created in the housing market.[4] There are also studies which, in contrast to Campbell and Mankiw (1991), report evidence suggesting that the link between consumption and current disposable income has become weaker in many countries following the liberalisation of financial markets; see Bayoumi (1993b) and Blundell-Wignall, Browne and Tarditi (1995).

---

[3] As suggested by Englund (1990), the idea that financial liberalisation caused the Swedish consumption boom may originate from the fact that the official forecasts of private consumption made by the National Institute of Economic Research showed unusually large underestimates for 1986 and 1987 — errors that were "explained" by financial deregulation.

[4] There are also some Swedish studies which indicate that housing prices and housing wealth affect consumption; see Agell, Berg and Edin (1995) and Berg and Bergström (1995). However, these findings do not necessarily imply that financial deregulation played a role. As pointed out by King (1990) and Pagano (1990), an increase in housing prices may stem from a variety of factors unrelated to the liberalisation of financial markets.

Although the bulk of the evidence seems to support the conventional argument that the deregulations did matter, our alternative reading of the data is not novel. King (1990) and Pagano (1990) both suggest that the U.K. consumption boom between 1986 and 1988 should be tied to permanent income dynamics rather than financial liberalisation. A recent interesting study by Attanasio and Weber (1994) exploits 15 waves (1974–88) of the U.K. *Family Expenditure Survey* to test various hypothesis about the decline in personal saving rates in the late 1980s. Attanasio and Weber find that housing price effects from financial liberalisation can account for a large part of observed changes in the intertemporal consumption pattern of older cohorts, but that the marked increase in spending levels of younger households, who contributed the most to the consumption boom, is best understood in terms of a revision of permanent income.

Section II takes a first look at the issues. We outline the time schedule of financial liberalisation, and we describe some of the important stylised facts of the Swedish boom-to-bust cycle. The belief that financial deregulation caused the consumption boom rests on the observation that consumption growth greatly outstripped income growth. We show, however, that conventionally defined disposable income understates the increase in aggregate wages during the boom years. Section III turns to the macro-econometric evidence. We find no evidence suggesting that consumption behaviour actually changed in the years following the liberalisation of financial markets. In our recursive regressions, the parameters that are supposed to capture the influence of liquidity constraints are remarkably stable until 1991, a finding which holds for different consumption aggregates. All our models, however, have a hard time tracking the development after 1991. There is strong evidence of parameter instability, and the parameter that we identify with liquidity constraints drifts upwards. The problems of drawing inferences about the importance of liquidity constraints from deviations from Euler conditions are well known, and we devote Section IV to a sensitivity analysis. Finally, Section V offers a few concluding remarks.

II. Some Stylised Facts

As was the case in many other countries, financial deregulation in Sweden was a drawn-out process, affecting different segments of financial markets at different times. Table 1 summarises some of the major steps.[5] Financial

---

[5] A full account of the liberalisation of Swedish financial markets is well beyond our scope. For a detailed treatment of financial deregualtion in Sweden, and a discussion of some of the internal and external driving forces, see Englund (1990).

Table 1. *Major steps in the liberalisation of Swedish financial markets*

Deregulation of bank deposit rates	1978–79
Deregulation of issuing private bond rates	1980
Deregulation of insurance companies' lending rates	1980
Abolishment of requirement that banks hold bonds	1983
Deregulation of banks' lending rates	May 1985
Loan ceiling on banks and finance companies lifted	Nov. 1985
Remaining foreign exchange controls lifted	1989

Source: Englund (1990).

deregulation started at a modest pace towards the end of the 1970s, and it was completed in 1989, when all remaining foreign exchange controls were lifted. As regards deregulations of direct relevance for household borrowing, most changes took place between 1983 and 1985. Abolishment of the requirements that banks hold bonds in 1983 implied that bank lending could be geared to the needs of new categories of borrowers, and the deregulation of banks' lending rates in May 1985 provided the prerequisite for a competitive market. Finally, the above-mentioned "November revolution" of the same year allowed banks and finance companies unlimited access to the household loan market.

Figure 1 plots the development of the average propensity to consume for three measures of per capita consumption during the Swedish boom-to-bust cycle: total consumption expenditures, expenditures on nondurable goods and services, and 'pure' consumption.[6] For all consumption measures, there was a marked increase in the consumption to disposable income ratio after the deregulations of 1985. The average propensity to consume for total consumption expenditures increased from 0.99 in 1985 to 1.05 in 1988. The exceptional decrease in the propensity to consume in the bust period after 1990 is also evident. As can be seen from Table 2, household indebtedness has evolved in a parallel manner. The ratio of gross household liabilities (including mortgage and consumer debt) to disposable income stood at 103 percent in 1985, reached a peak of 136 percent in 1989, and decreased to 92 percent in 1994.[7] Compared with the debt to income ratio, however, the ratio of debt to gross household wealth (including housing) shows a much less marked increase after 1985.

---

[6] Our data on nondurables consumption and total consumption expenditures come from the National Accounts. To arrive at a measure of pure consumption, we added an imputed figure for the service value of the stock of durables to the consumption of nondurable goods and services. Pure consumption is thus a measure which properly reflects the activity of consuming, as opposed to the activity of spending. See the Appendix for further details.

[7] An important qualification is that a part of the rapid debt increase after 1985 most likely reflects a shift away from borrowing not recorded in the National Accounts (i.e., borrowing that took place outside the balance sheets of financial institutions).

The sharp increase in the average propensity to consume constitutes the *prima facie* case for the view that consumption behaviour changed in the wake of financial deregulation. But some facts bark in another direction. A first observation is that the debt to income ratio increased from such a high initial level. The debt ratio in 1984, 105 percent does not fit neatly into a picture of widespread credit regulations.[8] Second, the argument of Muellbauer and Murphy (1990) that financial deregulation boosted consumption via induced wealth effects in the housing market implies that the consumption boom should coincide with a housing price boom. This does not quite

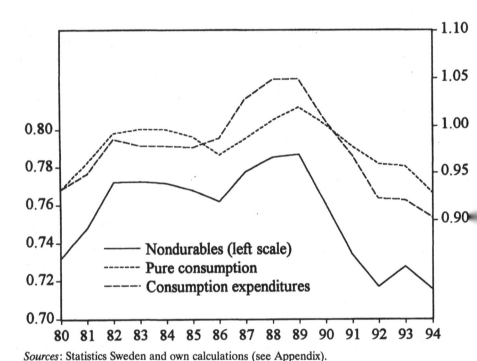

Sources: Statistics Sweden and own calculations (see Appendix).

Fig. 1. Average propensity to consume out of disposable income for three consumption measures, 1980–94.

---

[8] Comparable international figures for the period 1980–84 indicate that debt ratios were much lower in most other countries, ranging from 108, 82, 76 and 68 percent in Norway, Japan, the U.S. and the U.K., to 60, 50, 49 and 9 percent in France, Finland, Denmark and Italy. (Source: OECD Economic Outlook, 1994, and the National Accounts of the Nordic countries.)

fit the Swedish facts. The rapid increase in total consumption expenditures in 1986–87 actually *precedes* the housing market boom in 1988–89.[9]

Third, and most importantly, the increase in the average propensities to consume after 1985 reflects the combined effects of unusually large consumption growth rates, and unusually low disposable income growth rates. As can be seen from Table 2, disposable income actually decreased for three consecutive years after 1986. The important observation is that this decrease derives from nothing more than the accounting conventions of the National Accounts. Disposable income includes capital income, which is defined as the sum of dividends and net interest income. However, returns that materialise in the form of capital gains are not accounted for. In periods when households borrow to purchase assets like real estate and common stocks, i.e., assets for which capital gains are important components of the total return, this accounting procedure tends to understate income growth.[10] When we purge the disposable income measure of the

Table 2. *Growth rates of consumption and disposable income, and debt ratios (1980–94)*

	Per capita growth rates				Gross household debt to disposable income	Gross household debt to total private wealth
	Total consumption expenditures	Pure consumption	Nondurable consumption and services	Disposable income (Nat. Accounts)		
1980	−0.010	0.008	−0.006	0.026	0.981	0.219
1981	−0.003	0.009	0.001	−0.020	0.988	0.222
1982	0.007	0.001	0.000	−0.032	1.038	0.229
1983	−0.020	−0.009	−0.013	−0.013	1.037	0.228
1984	0.013	0.013	0.012	0.013	1.054	0.237
1985	0.025	0.018	0.022	0.026	1.033	0.233
1986	0.041	0.010	0.022	0.030	1.128	0.244
1987	0.041	0.018	0.020	−0.000	1.207	0.252
1988	0.019	0.019	0.009	−0.001	1.354	0.256
1989	−0.002	0.011	−0.001	−0.003	1.358	0.244
1990	−0.006	0.018	0.003	0.037	1.250	0.231
1991	0.003	0.017	0.005	0.040	1.079	0.216
1992	−0.020	0.009	0.005	0.029	1.007	0.212
1993	−0.043	−0.044	−0.027	−0.042	0.975	0.206
1994	−0.003	−0.011	0.000	0.017	0.916	0.199

Sources: Statistics Sweden and own calculations.

---

[9] Over the two years 1986 and 1987, general real housing prices increased by 10 percent; in 1988 and 1989, when the consumption boom was over, the corresponding figure was 23.7 percent (source: Statistics Sweden).

[10] For further discussions, see Agell, Berg and Edin (1995).

National Accounts of household capital income, a rather different picture emerges (see Appendix for details).

The solid curve in Figure 2, non-property income per capita, shows the development of the sum of wages, salaries and transfers minus direct taxes. Until the mid-1980s non-property income and disposable income evolved in a parallel manner, with three distinct trends: a steady increase until the mid-1970s, stagnation and decline between 1975 and 1983 — when Sweden like many other industrialised countries suffered from a prolonged recession — and a rebound thereafter. However, the rebound was much stronger for non-property income; between 1983 and 1989, non-property income increased by 13.3 percent, while conventionally defined disposable income increased by a mere 6.8 percent. During the same period total consumption expenditures, pure consumption and consumption of nondurables and services grew by 14.5, 9.3 and 8.8 percent, respectively. In short, the common belief that consumption growth greatly outstripped income growth in connection with financial deregulation is correct only if

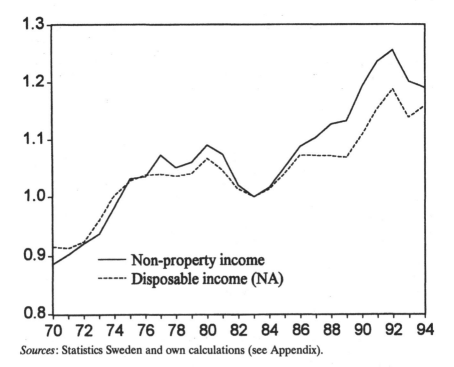

Sources: Statistics Sweden and own calculations (see Appendix).

Fig. 2. The development of two per capita income concepts, 1970–94 (index = 1, 1983).

the comparison is confined to an income concept which is subject to measurement errors.[11]

III. How has λ Evolved over Time?

Since the seminal work of Hall (1978) many researchers have adopted the Euler-equation approach to interpret the development of aggregate consumption over time. An important implication of the life-cycle/permanent-income model *cum* rational expectations hypothesis is that the consumption of households with access to a perfect capital market ought to follow a random walk. However, a common empirical finding is that consumption seems to respond to predictable changes in current income, i.e., there is evidence of "excess sensitivity". As one reason for excess sensitivity is the existence of liquidity-constraints, we would expect a link between the degree of excess sensitivity to the structure of financial institutions and regulations. With heavily regulated credit markets, consumption ought to track current income closely.[12]

In this section we examine the extent to which excess sensitivity has varied over time, using annual Swedish data since 1950. If the liberalisation of financial markets was important for consumption, we would expect to see a less tight relation between consumption and current income after the mid-1980s. For this purpose we use a model proposed by Campbell and Mankiw (1989, 1991) who extended the random walk model of consumption by assuming that there are two types of consumers in the economy. The first type obeys the logic of the life-cycle/permanent-income model, while the second sets spending equal to current income. Consider first the behaviour of a representative permanent-income household in the

---

[11] Although the macroeconomic pattern of wage income is of interest in its own right, microeconomic evidence suggests that the trend shift in wage growth after 1983 was unevenly distributed. As shown by Holmlund and Kolm (1995), real earnings after tax for the top quintile of the earnings distribution declined by 12.4 percent between 1975 and 1983, only to increase by 42 percent between 1983 and 1992. Thus, while most employees had reason to revise their perceptions of future labour income after 1983, certain segments of the work force ought to adjust more than others. In particular, highly skilled, and highly educated, consumers ought to account for a disproportionate share of the consumption boom. Although the popular press in the second half of the 1980s frequently ran stories about the conspicuous consumption of young urban professionals, there is unfortunately no solid microeconomic evidence on the incidence of Swedish consumption.

[12] Here, we follow many authors in adopting the maintained hypothesis that liquidity constraints are the reason for excess sensitivity. Under a standard alternative hypothesis, excess sensitivity rather reflects some kind of rule-of-thumb behaviour. There is no strong presumption as to how financial deregulation would affect the decision rules of rule-of-thumb households.

presence of a constant real interest rate. Under standard assumptions, the implied Euler equation can be approximated by the log-linear expression

$$\Delta c_t^p = \mu^* + \varepsilon_t^*, \tag{1}$$

where Δ is the first difference operator, c_t^p is the log of the consumption of permanent-income households in period t, μ^* is a constant, and ε_t^* is the error term, which represents news about permanent income. For current-income consumers, we have that

$$\Delta c_t^{ci} = \Delta y_t^{ci}, \tag{2}$$

where y_t^{ci} is the log of income of current-income consumers. If current-income consumers receive a constant share λ of total income, (1) and (2) imply that aggregate consumption is

$$\Delta c_t = \mu + \lambda \Delta y_t + \varepsilon_t, \qquad \cdot \tag{3}$$

where $\mu = (1 - \lambda) \mu^*$, $\varepsilon_t = (1 - \lambda) \varepsilon_t^*$, and y_t is the log of aggregate income.

As Δy_t will be correlated with ε_t, a consistent estimate of λ requires using instrumental variables techniques. The important problem concerns how the instruments should be dated. The theoretical model concerns consumption decisions that are made continuously, but available data represent time averages of consumption and income. Time averaging may then induce spurious first-order serial correlation in the error term, and hence a correlation between the contemporaneous error term and all once lagged instruments; see Hall (1988). The solution of Campbell and Mankiw is to rely on instruments dated $t - 2$ and earlier. A disadvantage of this conservative approach is that we lose predictive power in the first-stage regressions. It is much easier to forecast income growth if we have access to information dated $t - 1$. As instrumental variables techniques can be very unreliable when the instruments explain little of the variation in the endogenous r.h.s. variable, we follow Carroll, Fuhrer and Wilcox (1994) and estimate

$$\Delta c_t = \mu + \lambda \Delta y_t + v_t - \theta v_{t-1}. \tag{4}$$

The only difference between (4) and (3) lies in the treatment of the error term. As we estimate the moving average parameter directly, all instruments dated $t - 1$ should be orthogonal to the contemporaneous error v_t.[13]

We estimated (4) for the three different measures of per capita consumption displayed in Table 2, and our full annual data set stretches

---

[13] Additional virtue of the specification in (4) is that it accounts for the result of Mankiw (1982) that the change in spending ought to follow an MA(1) process when the consumption good is durable.

from 1950 to 1994.[14] As the Campbell-Mankiw model applies to the case where the consumption good is completely nondurable, our measure of the sum of expenditures on nondurable goods and services is the most appropriate left-hand variable. Our results for pure consumption and total consumption expenditures should be interpreted with care. In an economy which only consists of permanent-income consumers, a pure consumption measure is indeed quite appropriate. In an economy which only consists of current-income consumers, an expenditure based measure seems preferable. In an economy with a mixed population, neither consumption measure is quite defensible.

Another important data issue concerns the proper choice of right-hand variable in our regressions. As pointed out by Carroll, Fuhrer and Wilcox (1994), a literal interpretation of the Campbell-Mankiw model suggests that y_t should be identified with the kind of income actually received by current-income consumers. An implication of introducing consumers who always consume their income is that they do not build up assets, and that they do not receive capital income. In line with this observation, we identify y_t with the approximate measure of aggregate labour income per capita shown in Figure 2; i.e., non-property income.

Next, a few words about our instruments. It turns out that lagged income growth rates provide poor forecasts of current income growth. Over our full sample period, the adjusted R^2 statistic for forecasting income growth with its own lag is well below 10 percent. We obtain much better forecast equations when we include additional macroeconomic variables in the instrument set. In our benchmark set we include the first lag of income growth, and the corresponding lags of consumption growth, the change in real exports per capita, and the change in gross business investment per capita.

Table 3 presents our results for the sample period 1952–89, i.e., we quite deliberately exclude observations from the consumption bust of the 1990s.[15] Column 2 reports the adjusted R^2 statistic for the first-stage OLS regression of income growth on the instruments. In all three equations, adjusted R^2 is well above 35 percent. Columns 3 and 4 give the estimates of λ and the moving average parameter θ, with standard errors in parentheses. Column 5 reports the adjusted R^2 statistic for the regression, and column 6 shows a Sargan instrument validity test. At all conventional

---

[14] Although quarterly Swedish consumption data are available, we prefer to rely on annual data. After some preliminary experimentation with quarterly data, we found that our models were extremely sensitive to the choice of seasonal adjustment method. For further discussion of seasonality in aggregate Swedish consumption data, see Assarsson (1991).

[15] Although our data begin in 1950, we lose one observation when we move from levels to growth rates, and another observation due to the fact that all our instruments are lagged once.

Table 3. *Estimating the pure λ-model, $\Delta c_t = \mu + \lambda \Delta y_t + v_t - \theta v_{t-1}$ (1952–89)*

Consumption category	First-stage regr, $\bar{R}^2$	λ	θ	$\bar{R}^2$	Sargan test	$Q(2)$	ARCH LM(2)
Total consumption expenditures	0.360	0.521 (0.115)	0.353 (0.168)	0.266	0.34	0.39	0.71
Pure consumption	0.376	0.323 (0.081)	0.003 (0.169)	0.361	0.24	0.33	0.15
Nondurable goods and services	0.364	0.327 (0.103)	0.000 (0.175)	0.363	0.12	0.20	0.77

Notes: The estimation method is TSLS, and our software package is *EViews*, version 1.0. Our instrument set includes a constant, Δc_{t-1}, Δy_{t-1}, and the first lags of the logarithmic change in real exports and business fixed investment. Figures in parentheses are standard errors. The Sargan instrument test is asymptotically distributed as χ-square, and we report the probability value at which we can reject the null that the instruments are uncorrelated with the error term. The columns $Q(2)$ and ARCH LM(2) report the probability values for the Ljung-Box Q statistic for second-order serial correlation, and for the Lagrange multiplier test for autoregressive conditional heteroskedasticity (we included two lagged residuals). Both tests are asymptotically distributed as χ-square.

significance levels, there is no evidence against our instrument set. Finally, column 7 reports a test statistic for second-order serial correlation, and column 8 shows the ARCH LM statistic for heteroskedasticity.

Our estimates of λ are statistically significant, and of economic importance. The point estimates range from 0.52 for total consumption expenditures, to about 0.32 for spending on nondurables and pure consumption. Such marked — and not so easy to explain — differences in the estimates of λ across consumption categories with different relative durability are also reported by Carroll, Fuhrer and Wilcox (1994).[16] For pure consumption and nondurables, our estimates of the moving average parameter θ are close to zero, and statistically insignificant. For total consumption expenditures, θ is 0.353, with a standard error of 0.168.

Our estimates of λ for nondurables and pure consumption are very close to those reported by Campbell and Mankiw (1991). Using quarterly Swedish data on aggregate consumption of nondurables and services for the period 1972:1–1988:1, they obtain $\lambda = 0.35$. By contrast, Jappelli and Pagano (1989), who use annual data on consumption excluding expenditures on durables for the period 1965–83, report an insignificant point estimate of λ of 0.12. When we estimated our model for nondurables for

---

[16] As there are unresolved issues in the modelling of pure consumption and total consumption expenditures in the presence of liquidity constraints, we do not attach much economic substance to our diverging estimates of λ. However, under the assumption that current income consumers adopt a simple rule-of-thumb, Carroll, Fuhrer and Wilcox (1994) show that the estimate of λ will be biased upwards in direct proportion to the relative durability of the consumption category under study.

the same years we obtained $\lambda = 0.43$, with a standard error of 0.18. Preliminary experimentation on our part suggests that one important reason for the conflicting results might stem from the fact that Jappelli and Pagano ignore the problem of time aggregation. When we re-estimated the model without the moving average term, the point estimate of λ dropped to 0.25, which is no longer statistically significant (the standard error is 0.17).

The residuals for the critical years immediately after 1985 are of obvious interest. Somewhat to our surprise, the simple λ-models of Table 3 do not miss out very much during the consumption boom. The largest single positive errors for nondurables and pure consumption occur in 1987, when consumption growth is underpredicted by 0.6 and 0.2 percentage points, respectively. Once we control for the change in current income, there is in fact only a very small residual left to be accounted for by factors like permanent income revisions and financial liberalisation! Our residual for total consumption expenditures is another story. In 1986–87, when total consumption expenditures grew by more than four percent a year, our λ-model underpredicts consumption growth by 1.4 and 2.9 percentage points.[17]

Did excess sensitivity change in conjunction with the liberalisation of credit markets in the mid-1980s? There are many ways of looking for a change in the relation between consumption and income growth. Campbell and Mankiw (1991) examine whether λ is a linear function of time, and use a dummy variable test to see whether there was a structural break in the 1980s. Blundell-Wignall, Browne and Tarditi (1995) estimate separate λ equations for different time periods, and conclude that excess sensitivity became less pronounced in many countries during the 1980s. In the following we adopt a more visual approach. We calculate the recursive estimates of λ for each of our consumption aggregates, using the instrument set of Table 3. If the deregulations played a role, we would expect to see a downward jump in the point estimates of λ as we add observations from the 1980s.

Figure 3 plots the results from 1975 (i.e., a year when we have cumulated a decent number of degrees of freedom) and onwards. For pure consump-

---

[17] The large residuals for total consumption expenditures in 1986–87 reflect the fact that spending on durables grew rapidly in those years. One obvious interpretation is that financial deregulation mattered for durables spending, but not for nondurables purchases. But the residuals are also in line with the argument that permanent income revisions may have a disproportionate effect on the demand for luxury durable items, like boats and expensive cars. Another possibility, also unrelated to financial deregulation, is that large swings in durables purchases primarily reflect an optimal adjustment of irreversible investments to changes in perceived risk; see Hassler (1996) for analysis of the link between stock market risk and new car purchases in Sweden. In any case, the development of durables spending over the boom-to-bust cycle is an important topic for future research.

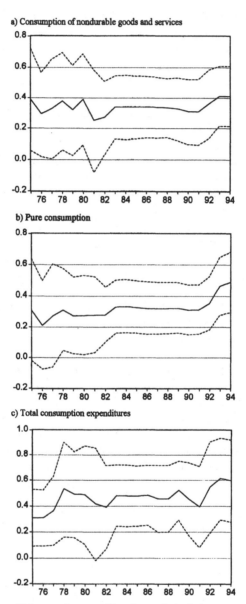

Fig. 3. Recursive coefficient estimates of lamda, and plus/minus two standard deviations (1975–94).

Notes: The sample begins in 1952, and we estimated equation (4) for nondurables, pure consumption and total consumption expenditures (all in per capita terms) with the instrument set of Table 3.

tion and spending on nondurable goods and services, the confidence intervals narrow when we extend the sample, but the point estimates of λ remain remarkably stable (slightly above 0.3) when we add observations for the 1980s. The same is true for the confidence intervals. For total consumption expenditures our λ estimates jump around more, and the confidence interval is typically much larger, but there is no evidence of decreasing excess sensitivity in the 1980s. Another observation is that the model digests the high growth rates for total consumption expenditures in 1986–87 without problem, in the sense that there is no indication of instability in λ. To the extent that excess sensitivity has something to say about liquidity constraints, we are left with the tentative conclusion that financial liberalisation in Sweden did little to alter the intertemporal trade-offs facing consumers. A substantial minority of households seemed to link their consumption to current income in the late 1970s, and the same was true ten years later.[18]

The development after 1991 is more puzzling — there is an *upward* drift in λ for all consumption measures. This finding is certainly in line with the popular argument that credit constraints became tighter in the wake of the deep recession, which forced the government to bail out some insolvent financial institutions. But there are other ways of interpreting this particular episode. A closer inspection of our data reveals that most of the instability in our λ estimates is driven by the observation for 1993. In that year, all variables took a sharp turn in the same direction: pure consumption, total consumption expenditures, nondurables consumption and current income decreased by 4.3, 4.4, 2.7 and 4.6 percent, respectively. However, after 1991 the macroeconomic environment, including the unemployment rate, changed dramatically. It is quite conceivable that the sharp fall in consumption in 1993 simply reflects a contemporaneous level ajdustment to increased uncertainty, rather than tighter credit constraints. When consumers are prudent, increased uncertainty boosts precautionary savings, which implies a drop in current consumption, and a higher consumption growth rate thereafter.[19]

IV. Some Extensions

Do our λ estimates, and their pattern over time, survive when we add some additional explanatory variables to equation (4)? Table 4 presents the

---

[18] We also conducted a number of Chow forecast tests to look for a structural break during the years of financial deregulation. For each of our consumption measures, we ran a series of tests, starting with the period 1982–89, and concluding with the period 1987–89. We found no sign of instability (these results can be provided on request).

[19] The simulations reported by Caballero (1991) indicate that small changes in perceived earnings uncertainty can have strong effects on current consumption.

results for three augmented models of λ for the period 1952–89. The first model allows for intertemporal substitution in response to a time-varying real interest rate after tax (rows 1, 4 and 7). The second builds on the idea that liquidity constraints may affect consumption growth via the change in the nominal interest rate; see e.g. Wilcox (1989). When banks evaluate credit worthiness in terms of the ratio between nominal debt services and nominal income, a higher nominal borrowing rate might imply that loan applications are denied more frequently (rows 2, 5 and 8).

Third, we also explore the possibility that there might be a long-run (cointegrating) relationship between consumption and various explanatory variables, in addition to the short run dynamics captured by (4).[20] A recent study on Swedish consumption by Berg and Bergström (1995) indicates that total consumption expenditures cointegrate with disposable income

Table 4. *Estimating augmented λ-models (1952–89):* $\Delta c_t = \mu + \lambda \Delta y_t + v_t - \theta v_{t-1} + \{ \beta_1 r_t \text{ or } \beta_2 \Delta i_t \text{ or } \beta_3 EC_{t-1} \}$

Row	Consumption category	λ	θ	β_1	β_2	β_3	$\bar{R}^2$	Sargan test	$Q(2)$	ARCH LM(2)
1	Total consumption expenditures	0.411 (0.107)	0.418 (0.166)	0.138 (0.071)	—	—	0.406	0.06	0.30	0.86
2	Total consumption expenditures	0.448 (0.097)	0.296 (0.175)	—	−0.501 (0.420)	—	0.424	0.16	0.15	0.53
3	Total consumption expenditures	0.315 (0.148)	−0.326 (0.224)	—	—	−0.462 (0.180)	0.343	0.15	0.41	0.35
4	Pure consumption	0.264 (0.081)	−0.003 (0.182)	0.076 (0.065)	—	—	0.410	0.05	0.63	0.09
5	Pure consumption	0.327 (0.088)	−0.003 (0.225)	—	−0.194 (0.397)	—	0.271	0.12	0.37	0.23
6	Pure consumption	Not applicable								
7	Nondurable goods and services	0.267 (0.086)	0.257 (0.180)	0.132 (0.061)	—	—	0.498	0.07	0.50	0.21
8	Nondurable goods and services	0.353 (0.095)	−0.003 (0.181)	—	−0.366 (0.365)	—	0.397	0.16	0.20	0.67
9	Nondurable goods and services	0.272 (0.102)	−0.237 (0.206)	—	—	−0.392 (0.141)	0.463	0.16	0.80	0.68

Notes: The estimation method is TSLS, and our software package is *EViews*, version 1.0. r_t is the real after-tax interest rate, Δi_t the change in the nominal borrowing interest rate, and EC_{t-1} the lagged error from a consumption function estimated in levels for the period 1951–89. The consumption function is in logs. Following the results of Berg and Bergström (1995) we let the right-hand variables include a constant, non-property income, and two wealth variables, net financial wealth and housing wealth (see Appendix). The augmented Dickey-Fuller test indicates that we can reject the hypothesis that EC_t has a unit root for total consumption expenditures and nondurables at the five percent level. Our basic instrument set is the same as in Table 3, appended with the lagged real interest rate when estimating β_1, the lagged change in the nominal interest rate when estimating β_2, and the lagged error-correction term when estimating β_3. Standard errors are in parentheses. For all other details, see the notes to Table 3.

---

[20] See e.g. Davidson, Hendry, Srba and Yeo (1978).

and household net wealth, once the wealth variable is diaggregated into financial and housing wealth. They also find that an error-correction term in the same variables may help to explain consumption growth. Our third model adds an error-correction term, EC_{t-1}, to equation (4). We estimate the levels relation between consumption, disposable income, financial net wealth and housing wealth, and identify the residual with the error-correction term.

We find evidence of a significant, but still fairly small, intertemporal elasticity of substitution for two of our consumption measures (total consumption expenditures and nondurables).[21] However, this effect disappears when we extend the sample period to 1994. Moreover, the Sargan test of the final column suggests that our instrument set does a poor job in all equations where we include the real after-tax interest rate. For all consumption aggregates, the change in the nominal borrowing rate has the expected negative sign. But the standard errors are large, and the coefficients are not even close to significant.[22]

Our error-correction specification is a mixed success. For pure consumption, we cannot reject the null that EC_t has a unit root. For total consumption expenditures and nondurables, however, the augmented Dickey-Fuller test indicates that we can reject the unit root hypothesis, which implies that EC_{t-1} is a legitimate error-correction term. As can be seen from rows 3 and 9, the error-correction terms for total consumption expenditures and nondurables are significant, and the negative signs are consistent with the conventional idea that disequilibrium dynamics may reduce consumption growth in times when the consumption level is relatively high.

For our purpose, the most interesting finding is that λ remains significant across all specifications, and that the point estimates are close to those reported for the basic model. Our finding of excess sensitivity does not seem to stem from inappropriate omission of obvious alternative variables. We also conducted a number of recursive regressions with our augmented models to look for jumps in λ during the 1980s.[23] As before, we found no indication of instability in the years immediately after financial deregulation, and again we found that λ started to drift upwards when we added observations after 1991.

---

[21] Technically, the parameter in front of the real interest rate is the product of the intertemporal elasticity of substitution and the fraction of permanent income households, $1 - \lambda$. The estimates in row 7 imply that the intertemporal elasticity of substitution is 0.18.

[22] By allowing for an interaction term between the level of the nominal interest rate and the rate of income growth, we also explored the idea that nominal interest rates may affect the share of households being liquidity constrained. However, the interaction term was not close to statistically significant for any of our three consumption measures.

[23] These results can be provided on request.

V. Concluding Remarks

Our case against the view that financial liberalisation in Sweden was an important event rests on three pieces of evidence. First, in an international comparison, Swedish households were heavily indebted long before the regulations were dismantled. There were also ways of avoiding the constraints implied by the formal rules. Second, the conventional view that consumption growth greatly outstripped income growth in the years after financial deregulation rests on a comparison with a less reliable disposable income concept. We show that the consumption boom was in fact accompanied by a trend shift in the growth of wage income. From this perspective, the Swedish consumption boom seems like a rather overrated puzzle. Third, if financial deregulation was important, current income ought to have become less important for consumption in the 1980s. But what we find is that not much happened. A substantial minority of households seemed to link their consumption to current income in the late 1970s, and the same was true ten years later.

There are often alternative ways of interpreting economic time series. Our pieces of evidence are circumstantial, and we do not want to give the impression that they allow us to reach a final verdict on financial deregulation in Sweden. We believe, though, that our investigation of the Swedish case raises some issues of more general interest.

First, in discussing the effects of financial liberalisation it is often forgotten that borrowing constraints may arise for a number of reasons other than government intervention. In the presence of asymmetric information, a standard theoretical result is that financial institutions may find it optimal to limit credit availability. In a situation where such equilibrium constraints bind, dismantling of the formal regulations need not have large effects. A better empirical understanding of the nature of equilibrium constraints, and how they interact with formal regulations, seems crucial.[24]

Second, while many countries liberalised their financial markets at the same time, we should not expect to see the same responses everywhere. Initial conditions are important; what matters a lot in country A might imply much less in country B. To our mind, much can be learned from case studies of the fine print and start-up conditions of financial liberalisation in individual countries.

---

[24] Models with endogenous liquidity constraints may have novel testable implications concerning the link between financial deregulation and excess sensitivity. Consider the following example, suggested by one of our referees. To the extent that Swedish households anticipated the rapid increase in income during the second half of the 1980s, an increased demand for borrowing ought to come forth. In a richer model, with endogenous liquidity constraints, this could possibly lead to more consumers becoming credit constrained, so that λ ought to increase. Our econometric finding that this did not happen could then be interpreted as suggesting that financial deregulation did matter.

Finally, deregulation may affect different margins of choice in different ways. Our conclusions that intertemporal consumption patterns were largely unaffected does not negate the possibility that changes took place along other dimensions, including investment patterns, asset choice and borrowing for commercial purposes.

Appendix. Data Sources

Table A1. Time series used in the estimations of Sections III and IV. All variables except the interest rates, REALR and NOMR, are expressed in per capita terms and 1991 prices

	YDNP	CPF	CP	CPND	WH	WFN	REALR	NOMR	INV	EXPORT
1950	31750	43395	43528	36340	96843	10593	# N/A	0.035	9767	7722
51	31809	42885	42705	35309	90826	11568	−0.099	0.035	9868	8175
52	34066	43810	44283	36751	90927	11492	−0.045	0.035	9890	7538
53	34944	44216	45114	37445	92864	11855	0.004	0.035	10848	7770
54	35570	45278	46695	38595	95988	14649	0.005	0.035	12116	8550
55	37545	46473	47853	39762	100457	14178	−0.007	0.047	11857	8945
56	37623	47419	48838	40483	102883	14354	−0.023	0.048	12128	9711
57	37879	47831	49255	40599	103230	14760	−0.008	0.055	12171	10512
58	38503	48650	50128	41238	103766	16036	−0.013	0.058	13124	10447
59	38627	49800	51652	42113	107738	20615	0.014	0.057	14387	11022
1960	40761	50949	52224	42890	109636	20916	−0.010	0.061	15186	12323
61	43626	52869	54744	44556	115464	21914	0.006	0.061	16480	12903
62	46488	54744	56983	46162	121479	21607	−0.014	0.052	17536	14052
63	48565	55776	58409	47046	118637	24660	−0.007	0.052	17986	14802
64	50692	57660	60382	48167	129252	27098	−0.010	0.058	19112	16483
65	50932	59019	61773	48929	132962	27755	−0.021	0.070	19493	17077
66	51737	60096	62403	49922	141391	23957	−0.033	0.074	20171	17746
67	51653	61364	63427	50873	146729	28012	−0.025	0.069	20838	18606
68	53691	63307	65713	52467	156923	37490	0.010	0.072	20356	19925
69	55691	65223	68004	53923	165219	44449	−0.002	0.082	21008	22008

Table A1. *continued*

	YDNP	CPF	CP	CPND	WH	WFN	REALR	NOMR	INV	EXPORT
1970	57710	67667	69712	55760	183322	38527	−0.014	0.089	21293	23684
71	58763	67963	69480	55873	187180	39027	−0.043	0.081	21510	24709
72	60000	69006	71743	57270	191873	37116	−0.043	0.073	22530	26113
73	61036	70375	73455	58148	197401	32324	−0.051	0.074	23593	29634
74	63966	71633	75636	58870	198956	30058	−0.076	0.088	22871	31084
75	67137	74277	77735	60411	196853	30328	−0.076	0.094	23683	27908
76	67374	76197	80399	62060	203266	24035	−0.082	0.092	24193	29203
77	69885	76984	79266	61639	211525	23493	−0.071	0.112	22557	29518
78	68408	77089	78540	61387	218658	21766	−0.082	0.102	20893	31754
79	69047	78876	80258	62722	226268	21169	−0.046	0.105	21975	33627
1980	70980	79473	79473	62378	218771	23808	−0.077	0.136	22781	33353
81	69945	80189	79220	62465	198237	34095	−0.068	0.170	21318	34022
82	66396	80247	79749	62472	191401	34683	−0.054	0.170	21273	35974
83	65115	79561	78134	61691	179387	44325	−0.057	0.155	21575	39480
84	66159	80589	79170	62422	177671	38611	−0.024	0.165	23421	42107
85	68470	82091	81140	63789	178346	45167	−0.017	0.185	24959	42623
86	70804	82937	84496	65220	182503	56499	−0.010	0.155	25058	44088
87	71836	84443	88007	66542	194592	47852	−0.017	0.123	27241	45787
88	73376	86041	89670	67152	219260	50382	−0.018	0.133	28906	46682
89	73743	86986	89465	67098	239091	53344	−0.024	0.138	31953	47748
1990	77640	88560	88959	67300	258007	39033	−0.044	0.162	32241	48165
91	80562	90083	89229	67632	250452	38250	−0.041	0.147	28584	46758
92	81885	90903	87495	67966	236614	46312	0.038	0.161	24908	47591
93	78235	86979	83773	66163	203275	66716	−0.018	0.121	19555	50894
94	77489	85989	83521	66189	197011	70424	0.003	0.106	19042	57465

The sources are the National and Financial Accounts of Statistics Sweden, if otherwise not stated.

YDNP   Nonproperty disposable income. Constructed after excluding household capital income and the operating surplus for unincorporated businesses and real estate from the disposable income measure of the National Accounts.

CPF   Pure consumption. Defined as expenditures on nondurable goods and services, plus the value of services generated from the stock of durables owned by households. In constructing the stock of durables, we started out with 1950 benchmark values for cars, other durables and semi-durables, and proceeded by employing the perpetual inventory method. The depreciation rates for each of the three categories of durables were set at 0.1, 0.15 and 0.3, respectively. In any period t, the consumption value for each durable category is defined as

$$\frac{(i(1-m)+\delta)P_K K}{P},$$

where i is the nominal lending rate, m a marginal tax rate, δ the geometric depreciation rate, P_K the price index for new durables in the relevant category, K the durables stock, and P a general price index.

CP   Total private consumption expenditures.

CPND   Expenditures on nondurable goods and services.

WH   Housing wealth. Defined as the market value of owner-occupied homes and vacation houses. Both WH and WFN are developed from Berg (1988).

WFN   Financial net wealth. Includes the sum of deposits, corporate shares (at market value), bonds, assets in pension funds (voluntary life insurance savings), other financial assets, minus loans.

REALR   Real after-tax interest rate. We calculated the nominal lending rate after tax, and adjusted for *ex post* inflation over the year. The marginal tax rate is the average marginal tax rate of white-collar workers, calculated by Du Rietz (1994).

NOMR   The nominal borrowing rate. Our source for 1950–88 is the Association of Swedish Savings Banks, and for 1989–94 the Riksbank.

INV   Gross business investment.

EXPORT   Value of exports of goods and services.

References

Agell, J., Berg, L. and Edin, P.-A.: The Swedish boom to bust cycle: Tax reform, consumption and asset structure. *Swedish Economic Policy Review 2*, 273–314, 1995.

Assarsson, B.: The stochastic behaviour of durables and nondurables consumption in Sweden. WP 1991:21, Department of Economics, Uppsala University, 1991.

Attanasio, O. P. and Weber, G.: The UK consumption boom of the late 1980s: Aggregate implications of microeconomic evidence. *Economic Journal 104*, 1269–302, 1994.

Bayoumi, T.: Financial deregulation and household saving. *Economic Journal 103*, 1432–43, 1993a.

Bayoumi, T.: Financial deregulation and consumption in the United Kingdom. *Review of Economics and Statistics 75*, 536–9, 1993b.

Berg, L.: *Hushållens sparande och konsumtion* (Household Saving and Consumption). Allmänna Förlaget, Stockholm, 1988.

Berg, L.: Household savings and debts: The experience of the Nordic countries. *Oxford Review of Economic Policy 10*, 42–52, 1994.

Berg, L. and Bergström, R.: Housing and financial wealth, financial deregulation and consumption — the Swedish case. *Scandinavian Journal of Economics 97*, 421–39, 1995.

Blundell-Wignall, A., Browne, F. and Tarditi, A.: Financial liberalization and the permanent income hypothesis. *The Manchester School 63*, 125–44, 1995.

Caballero, R. J.: Earnings uncertainty and aggregate wealth accumulation. *American Economic Review 81*, 859–71, 1991.

Campbell, J. Y. and Mankiw, N. G.: Consumption, income, and interest rates: Reinterpreting the time series evidence. In O. J. Blanchard and S. Fischer (eds.), *NBER Macroeconomics Annual 1989*, MIT Press, Cambridge, MA, 1989.

Campbell, J. Y. and Mankiw, N. G.: The response of consumption to income: A cross-country investigation. *European Economic Review 35*, 723–67, 1991.

Carroll, C. D., Fuhrer, J. C. and Wilcox, D. W.: Does consumer sentiment forecast hosuehold spending? If so, why? *American Economic Review 84*, 1397–408, 1994.

Davidson, J. E. H., Hendry, D. F., Srba, F. and Yeo, S.: Econometric modelling of the aggregate time-series relationship between consumer's expenditure and income in the United Kingdom. *Economic Journal 88*, 661–92, 1978.

Du Rietz, G.: *Välfärdsstatens finansiering* (Financing the Welfare State). City University Press, Stockholm, 1994.

Englund, P.: Financial deregulation in Sweden. *European Economic Review 34*, 385–93, 1990.

Hall, R.: Stochastic implications of the life cycle-permanent income hypothesis: Theory and evidence. *Journal of Political Economy 86*, 971–87, 1978.

Hall, R.: Intertemporal substitution in consumption. *Journal of Political Economy 96*, 339–57, 1988.

Hassler, J.: Risk and consumption. Forthcoming in *Swedish Economic Policy Review*, 1996.

Holmlund, B. and Kolm, A.-S.: Progressive taxation, wage setting, and unemployment: Theory and Swedish evidence. *Swedish Economic Policy Review 2*, 425–60, 1995.

Jappelli, T. and Pagano, M.: Consumption and capital market imperfections: An international comparison. *American Economic Review 79*, 1088–1105, 1989.

Jonung, L.: Riksbankens politik 1945–1990 (Policy of the Bank of Sweden, 1945–1990). In L. Werin (ed.), *Från räntereglering till inflationsnorm* (From Regulating Interest Rates to an Inflationary Norm), SNS Förlag, Stockholm, 1993.

King, M.: Discussion. *Economic Policy 11*, 383–7, 1990.

Koskela, E., Loikkanen, H. and Virén, M.: House prices, household saving and financial market liberalization in Finland. *European Economic Review 36*, 549–58, 1992.

Mankiw, G.: Hall's consumption hypothesis and durable goods. *Journal of Monetary Economics 15*, 417–26, 1982.

Miles, D.: Housing markets, consumption and financial liberalisation in the major economies. *European Economic Review 36*, 1093–1136, 1992.

Muellbauer, J. and Murphy, A.: Is the UK balance of payments sustainable? *Economic Policy 11*, 345–83, 1990.

Pagano, M.: Discussion. *Economic Policy 11*, 387–90, 1990.

Wilcox, J. A.: Liquidity constraints on consumption: The real effects of "real" lending policies. *Federal Reserve Bank of San Francisco Economic Review*, no. 4, 39–52, 1989.

Inviting Excess Volatility? Opening Up a Small Stock Market to International Investors

*Peter Sellin**

Sveriges Riksbank, S-103 37 Stockholm, Sweden

Abstract

What is the effect on asset prices of opening up a small stock market to international investors? In this paper some evidence is found that net purchases of stocks by foreign investors lead to temporary price effects in a small stock market. On average, foreign investors' net purchases of stocks look like noise trading and seem to create some amount of excess volatility in the market.

I. Introduction

In recent years we have witnessed a strong move towards international capital market liberalization. While the benefits of international diversification are widely recognized, some concern has also been expressed about opening up a small market to international investors. These concerns are most often voiced by managers, trade union representatives, and politicians in the small country. The gist of the argument is that international investors are short-sighted and move large amounts of funds in and out of a country's stock market with no regard to fundamentals. This myopic behavior is claimed to create excess volatility in the market.

The case of Sweden provides us with a unique set of data for assessing whether there is any foundation for these concerns. The removal of restrictions on foreign ownership of Swedish stocks on January 1, 1993, has led to a dramatic increase in trading in Swedish stocks by foreign investors.[1] The

---

*I am grateful to Magnus Dahlquist, Sonja Daltung, Per Jannson, Anders Warne, two anonymous referees, and the participants at seminars at the Institute for International Economic Studies (IIES) and Sveriges Riksbank for useful comments on an earlier version of this paper and to Magnus Forsells for providing me with the data. Some of the work on this paper was done while I was a research fellow at the IIES, Stockholm University. The views expressed here are those of the author and do not necessarily reflect those of Sveriges Riksbank.

[1] Before January 1, 1993, foreign ownership in a Swedish company was limited to 20% of the voting rights or 40% of the equity. The constraints were implemented by requiring firms allowing foreign ownership to issue a class of "unrestricted stocks", that could be held by both foreign and domestic investors, along with a class of "restricted stocks" that could only be held by Swedish investors. See Bergström, Rydqvist and Sellin (1993) for an analysis of the effects of these restrictions.

share of the Swedish stock market held by foreign investors has increased from around 10% before January 1, 1993, to over 30% today (April 1996). Do foreign investors behave in a myopic fashion or do they trade on the basis of information about fundamentals? Do these international trades create excess volatility in the Swedish stock market? This paper aims to answer these questions.

We consider two contrasting ways of characterizing the average trading behavior of international investors: *informational trading* and *noise trading*.

Informational trading is the traditional way of thinking about trading in financial economics. The only reason for agents to trade is the arrival of new information. According to conventional financial theory, all new publicly available information is rapidly impounded in securities prices through trading by informed investors. Securities markets are said to be informationally efficient, or semistrong-form efficient in the terminology of Fama (1970). Even private information seems to be fairly rapidly impounded in securities prices through trading by insiders; see e.g. Fama (1991). "Insider" is sometimes interpreted broadly to include agents with a superior analytical capability. It is certainly possible that some of the large foreign investors who are active in the Swedish stock market could possess such an analytical capability.

Noise trading is trading that is not based on information about fundamentals. In his presidential address to the American Finance Association, Fisher Black (1986), warned the profession that uninformed investors could introduce a nonnegligible amount of noise in the market. A formal model with informed traders and noise traders was developed by Kyle (1985). Noise traders trade for some reason that is unknown to the model builder and is thus represented as noise.[2] The informational efficiency of the market then depends on the extent to which there are noise traders in the market.

The following hypotheses are tested:

1. *Informational trading hypothesis.* Foreign investors' trading in the Swedish stock market is best characterized as informational trading. That is, information about fundamentals, possessed by foreign investors, is rapidly impounded in stock prices as the stocks are being traded by these investors. Thus, data on trading by foreign investors in previous periods

---

[2] Even though noise traders may look like uninformed traders, they may trade for some perfectly rational reason. See e.g. the model in Drees and Eckwert (1995), where preferences are such that current consumption affects the investor's attitudes toward risk in the future. Other non-informational reasons for trading are discussed in Grossman (1995).

should have no value in predicting current returns, since the information that trading was based on is already reflected in today's stock price.

2. *Noise trading hypothesis.* Foreign investors' trading in the Swedish stock market is best characterized as noise trading. That is, what mainly drives foreign trading is not information about fundamentals. If foreign trading is relatively large, then these trades could move Swedish stock prices away from their fundamental values. However, this would create an incentive for informed investors to enter the market and trade until the fundamental values have been restored. Hence, foreign trading can have temporary price effects and data on trading by foreign investors in previous periods may help predict current returns.

The noise trading hypothesis implies that trading causes stock prices to change, but that prices later revert to their fundamental values. On the other hand, the informational trading hypothesis implies that trading has a permanent effect on prices. Thus, positive effects of trading on returns should be followed by negative effects in later periods according to the noise trading hypothesis, while there should be only a simultaneous effect according to the informational trading hypothesis. None of the hypotheses implies reverse causality from returns to trading. It thus seems natural to start the analysis by establishing the direction of causality. We then estimate a regression model and conduct some formal tests in order to distinguish between the two hypotheses.

The plan of the paper is as follows. The data are presented in the next section. In Section III we apply Granger causality tests to establish the direction of causality between trading and returns. In Section IV we formally test the informational trading hypothesis versus the noise trading hypothesis. Section V concludes.

II. Data Description and Definitions of Variables

All data used in this study are from Sveriges Riksbank (the Swedish central bank). Monthly data on purchases (P_t) and sales (S_t) of Swedish stocks by foreign investors are available from Sveriges Riksbank starting in July 1983. The period studied is July 1983 to June 1995. From Figures 1 and 2 it is clear that foreign interest in the Swedish stock market has increased dramatically since January 1, 1993.

For this study the variable of interest is net purchases of Swedish stocks by foreign investors $(P_t - S_t)$. In Figure 3 net purchases are shown along with the Stockholm Stock Exchange Index, I_t. These series are clearly nonstationary. To get a stationary series of net purchases, we normalize by dividing net purchases by total turnover (by foreigners), giving us the variable $x_t = (P_t - S_t)/(P_t + S_t)$. Monthly returns on the stock index,

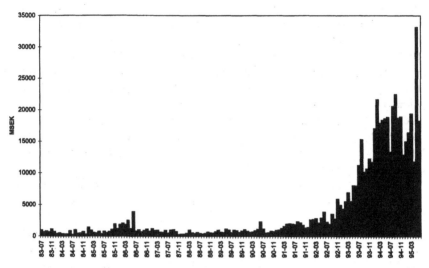

Fig. 1. Purchases of Swedish stocks by foreign investors, 1983:7–1995:6.

$r_t = \log (I_t/I_{t-1})$, have been plotted along with net purchases over turnover in Figure 4. There is no evidence of nonstationarity in either of these series (we will formally test this in the next section). The average monthly return for the period was 1%. Foreign investors were net buyers of Swedish equity during the period, as reflected in a monthly average of 0.08 for the net

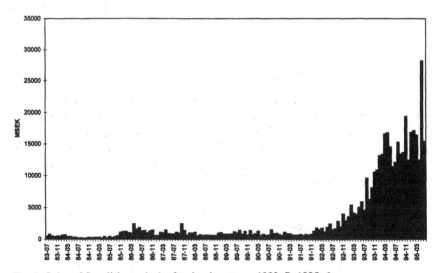

Fig. 2. Sales of Swedish stocks by foreign investors, 1983:7–1995:6.

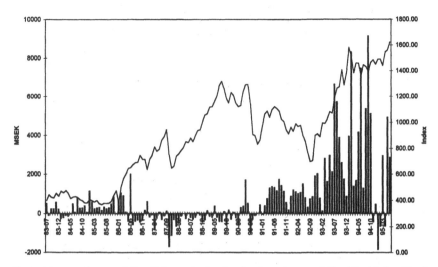

Fig. 3. Net purchases of Swedish stocks by foreign investors and the Stockholm Stock Exchange index, 1983:7–1995:6.

purchase over turnover variable x_t. We may also want to consider the effects of purchases and sales separately. For this reason we define the following purchase and sales variables, $p_t = \log(P_t/(P_t + S_t))$ and $s_t = \log(S_t/(P_t + S_t))$.

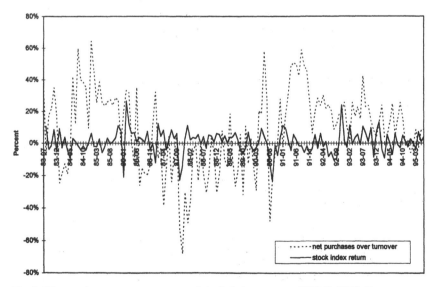

Fig. 4. Net purchases over turnover and stock index returns, 1983:8–1995:6.

III. Granger Causality Tests

We now determine the direction of causality between trading and returns as a preliminary step in our analysis. We use the concept of Granger causality.

The variable z_t is said *not* to Granger cause y_t if the lagged variables z_{t-i}, $i = 1, ..., m$ have no explanatory power in the following regression.

$$y_t = c + \sum_{i=1}^{m} \alpha_i y_{t-i} + \sum_{i=1}^{m} \beta_i z_{t-i} + \varepsilon_t. \tag{1}$$

Hence, if the restriction $\beta_i = 0$, $i = 1, ..., m$ is rejected, we say that z_t Granger causes y_t. The variables used in the tests should be stationary. Dickey-Fuller tests were therefore performed on r_t, x_t, p_t, and s_t. The presence of a unit root could be rejected at the 1% level in all cases.

Before we consider whether trading Granger causes returns or not, we want to make sure that causality does not run in the reverse direction. We thus check if returns Granger cause trading using the Granger regression

$$x_t = c + \sum_{i=1}^{m} \alpha_i x_{t-i} + \sum_{i=1}^{m} \beta_i r_{t-i} + \varepsilon_t. \tag{2}$$

We also allow for the possibility of asymmetric behavior of purchases and sales by using p_t and s_t instead of x_t in the regression above.

The Granger causality tests are reported in Table 1.[3] The probability values for the F-tests with regard to net purchases, purchases, and sales are

Table 1. *Granger causality tests: do returns Granger cause trading?*

Dependent Variable	Independent Variables	Lags	F-test: $\beta_i = 0$, all i
x_t	r_{t-i}	$i = 1, 2, 3.$	1.479 (0.223)
p_t	r_{t-i}	$i = 1, ..., 7.$	1.314 (0.249)
s_t	r_{t-i}	$i = 1, 2.$	0.819 (0.443)

Notes: F-tests with probability values in parentheses. The number of lags are based on Akaike's FPE criterion.

---

[3] The number of lags in the reported F-tests are based on Akaike's final prediction error (FPE) criterion. However, F-tests for all lags between those given by the Schwartz (SC) and Akaike (AIC) information criteria (usually 1–8 lags) were computed and gave qualitatively the same results as those reported in the table. See Judge *et al.* (1985) for a discussion of the criteria used.

Table 2. *Granger causality tests: does trading Granger cause returns?*

Dependent Variable	Independent Variables	Lags	F-test: $\beta_i = 0$, all i
r_t	x_{t-i}	$i = 1, 2.$	2.882 (0.038)
r_t	p_{t-i}	$i = 1, 2.$	3.779 (0.012)
r_t	s_{t-i}	$i = 1, 2.$	2.261 (0.084)

Notes: F-tests with probability values in parentheses. The number of lags are based on Akaike's FPE criterion.

all greater than 0.22. Hence, we cannot reject the hypothesis that returns do not Granger cause trading.

We now consider the reverse Granger causality associated with (2), which is consistent with the informational trading and the noise trading hypothesis. We estimate the following model:

$$r_t = c + \sum_{i=1}^{m} \alpha_i r_{t-i} + \sum_{i=0}^{m} \beta_i z_{t-i} + \varepsilon_t, \qquad (3)$$

where z_t is x_t, p_t, and s_t. The results of the causality tests are shown in Table 2.[4] We reject the hypothesis that trading does not Granger cause returns at the 10% significance level in all three cases (and at the 5% level in two cases). Thus, causality seems to run in the direction predicted by the informational trading and the noise trading hypotheses.

IV. Informational Trading or Noise Trading?

In order to be able to distinguish between the informational trading and the noise trading hypotheses, we have to take a closer look at the estimated models. The estimates are presented in Table 3. According to the informational trading hypothesis, returns should not be influenced by trades in previous periods. However, the restrictions $\beta_1 = \beta_2 = 0$ is rejected at the 5% significance level for all three model specifications.[5]

---

[4] Akaike's FPE criterion chose two lags in all three cases. The Akaike information criterion also suggested two lags in all three cases, while the conservative Schwartz criterion instead proposed one lag in two cases.

[5] Even though the White heteroskedasticity-consistent covariance estimator has inflated the standard errors, we cannot be too confident about the inference since the distribution is clearly leptokurtic according to a Bera-Jarque test (not reported). As an alternative to the White correction for general forms of heteroskedasticity, an ARCH(1) model was specified. The quasi maximum likelihood approach of Bollerslev and Wooldridge (1992) was applied. However, the ARCH parameter in the estimated model proved not to be significant, suggesting that some other form of heteroskedasticity is present.

A formal test of the noise trading hypothesis is a test of the restrictions that $\beta_0 = \beta_1 = \beta_2 = 0$ and $\beta_0 + \beta_1 + \beta_2 = 0$. If the noise trading hypothesis is true, we should reject the first restriction but fail to reject the second. Through the Granger causality tests we have already established that the first restriction does not hold. From Table 3 it is clear that we cannot reject the second restriction for any of the three models. Thus, foreign net purchases only have a temporary effect on Swedish stock prices. A similar result was obtained in a previous version of this paper for the shorter

Table 3. *Tests of purchases and sales of Swedish stocks by foreign investors as informational trading or noise trading. The estimated model is*

$$r_t = c + \alpha_1 r_{t-1} + \alpha_2 r_{t-2} + \beta_0 z_t + \beta_1 z_{t-1} + \beta_2 z_{t-2} + \varepsilon_t.$$

$z_t = x_t$	α_1	α_2	β_0	β_1	β_2
Estimate	0.066	−0.044	0.028	0.054	−0.085
t-statistic	(0.792)	(0.523)	(0.921)	(1.580)	(2.777)
t-statistic (White)	[0.586]	[0.481]	[0.717]	[1.401]	[2.646]

$Q(9) = 4.18\,(0.899),\ R^2_{adj} = 0.03$

Info trading:
$H_0: \beta_1 = \beta_2 = 0$ 3.916 (0.022) [0.028]
Noise trading:
$H_0: \beta_0 + \beta_1 + \beta_2 = 0$ 0.005 (0.942) [0.931]

$z_t = p_t$	α_1	α_2	β_0	β_1	β_2
Estimate	0.059	−0.035	0.036	0.056	−0.086
t-statistic	(0.711)	(0.425)	(1.257)	(1.748)	(3.027)
t-statistic (White)	[0.529]	[0.387]	[0.898]	[1.489]	[3.159]

$Q(9) = 3.89\,(0.918),\ R^2_{adj} = 0.05$

Info trading:
$H_0: \beta_1 = \beta_2 = 0$ 4.676 (0.011) [0.006]
Noise trading:
$H_0: \beta_0 + \beta_1 + \beta_2 = 0$ 0.053 (0.819) [0.788]

$z_t = s_t$	α_1	α_2	β_0	β_1	β_2
Estimate	0.064	−0.044	−0.026	−0.033	0.067
t-statistic	(0.759)	(0.524)	(0.963)	(1.117)	(2.530)
t-statistic (White)	[0.550]	[0.483]	[0.873]	[1.067]	[2.462]

$Q(9) = 3.94\,(0.915),\ R^2_{adj} = 0.02$

Info trading:
$H_0: \beta_1 = \beta_2 = 0$ 3.200 (0.044) [0.038]
Noise trading:
$H_0: \beta_0 + \beta_1 + \beta_2 = 0$ 0.120 (0.729) [0.654]

Notes: $Q(9)$ is the Ljung-Box statistic for serial correlation (probability value in parentheses). In connection with the F-tests of the hypotheses, probability values are shown in parentheses and probability values based on White's (1980) heteroskedasticity-consistent covariance matrix estimator are in square brackets. The intercept is not reported due to space considerations.

period June 1985 to June 1992, using a stock market index for unrestricted stocks; see Sellin (1994). In contrast to restricted stocks, unrestricted stocks could be held by foreign investors (cf. footnote 1). In the earlier paper the point estimates were also close to summing to zero to three decimal places. Thus, this finding seems to be quite robust to the sample period and stock index used.

The estimated models are consistent with the following story. Foreign investors buy (sell) Swedish stocks causing prices to rise (fall). Prices continue to rise (fall) in the following month, but in the month after that they fall (rise) back to about the same level as before the buying (selling) started. This interpretation supports the noise trading hypothesis that foreign investors temporarily push up (down) prices as they move into (out of) the Swedish stock market. If foreign investors entered and exited the Swedish market based on news about fundamentals, the price changes should be permanent, which they are not.

There is, of course, an alternative explanation which says that, on average, foreign investors correctly anticipate the direction of the market and quickly move in and out of the market (within three months) to take advantage of temporary movements in prices. However, this explanation does not seem very realistic. It is also not consistent with the positive serial correlation in the net purchase series.

Taken together, the evidence presented in this section is in favour of accepting the noise trading hypothesis. Net purchases of Swedish stocks by foreign investors have only a temporary price pressure effect. The price impact is reversed within three months.

V. Conclusions

We have investigated the relationship between a price index of Swedish stocks and the net purchases of Swedish stocks by foreign investors. There is some evidence in favor of the noise trading hypothesis. The analysis shows that the impact of net purchases by foreign investors on stock prices is only temporary. The price impact over the first two months is reversed in the third month. Thus, on average, foreign investors' net purchases of Swedish stocks look like noise trading, rather than informational trading, and seem to create some amount of excess volatility in the market.

References

Black, F.: Noise. *Journal of Finance 41*, 529–43, 1986.
Bergström, C., Rydqvist, K. and Sellin, P.: Asset pricing with in- and outflow constraints — theory and empirical evidence from Sweden. *Journal of Business Finance and Accounting 20*, 865–79, 1993.

Bollerslev, T. and Wooldridge, J.: Quasi-maximum likelihood estimation and inference in dynamic models with time-varying covariances. *Econometric Reviews 11*, 143–72, 1992.

Drees, B. and Eckwert, B.: The composition of stock price indices and the excess volatility puzzle. *International Review of Economics and Finance 4*, 29–36, 1995.

Engle, R.: Autoregressive conditional heteroskedasticity with estimates of the variance of U.K. inflation. *Econometrica 50*, 987–1008, 1982.

Fama, E.: Efficient capital markets — a review of theory and empirical work. *Journal of Finance 25*, 383–417, 1970.

Fama, E.: Efficient capital markets II. *Journal of Finance 46*, 1575–617, 1991.

Grossman, S.: Dynamic asset allocation and the informational efficiency of markets. *Journal of Finance 50*, 773–87, 1995.

Judge, G. G., Griffiths, W. E., Hill, R. C., Lutkepohl, H. and Lee, T. C.: *The Theory and Practice of Econometrics*, Second edition, John Wiley & Sons, New York, 1985.

Kyle, A.: Continuous auctions and insider trading. *Econometrica 53*, 1315–35, 1985.

Sellin, P.: Do foreign investors have a market impact on Swedish stock prices? Institute for International Economic Studies WP 581, University of Stockholm, 1994.

White, H.: A heteroskedasticity-consistent covariance matrix estimator and a direct test for heteroskedasticity. *Econometrica 48*, 817–38, 1980.

Index